SALZBURG TRAVEL GUIDE 2023 AND BEYOND

Your Ultimate Guide To Explore the Best of Mozart's Hometown

By: Leon Jonas

Copyright © 2023 Leon Jonas

All rights reserved.

Without the proper written consent of the publisher and copyright owner, this book cannot be used or distributed in any way, shape, or form, except for brief quotations used in a review. This book should not be considered a substitute for medical, legal, or other professional advice.

Contents

INTRODUCTION	1
THE HISTORY OF SALZBURG	4
Prehistory and Ancient Times	4
Early Middle Ages	5
Salzburg as an Independent Principality	5
Reformation and Counter-Reformation	5
18th Century and Mozart	6
Napoleon's Influence	6
20th Century and World War II	6
2023 and Beyond	6
TRAVEL PRACTICALITIES	7
Visa and Travel Documents for Austria	7
Best Time to Visit Salzburg	9
How to Get to Salzburg	11
Getting Around Salzburg	13
Accommodation in Salzburg	15
Shopping in Salzburg	17
Health and Safety	20
Currency and Payments	23
Travel Insurance	25
Packing Essentials	26
Language	28

Electrical Outlets	29
Emergency Numbers	29
Local Customs and Etiquette	30
Internet and Communication	32
ACTIVITIES	34
Boat Rides	34
Take a Day Trip	37
Outdoor Activities	40
Nightlife in Salzburg	43
Family-Friendly Activities	45
Visit Christmas Markets	47
Shopping	50
Attend a Festive Event	52
Strolls and Hikes	55
TOP ATTRACTIONS IN SALZBURG	58
Salzburg Old Town (Altstadt)	58
Hohensalzburg Fortress	62
Mozarts Geburtshaus (Mozart's Birthplace)	65
Mirabell Palace and Gardens	68
Salzburg Cathedral (Salzburger Dom)	71
Mozarts Wohnhaus (Mozart's Residence)	74
Hellbrunn Palace and Trick Fountains	77
St. Peter's Abbey and Cemetery	79

Kapitelplatz and Giant Chess Board	82
Salzburg Tree Tunnel	84
HIDDEN GEMS	86
Petersfriedhof Cemetery	86
Nonnberg Abbey	89
Müllner Bräu Brewery & Beer Garden	92
Stieglkeller	94
Kaffee-Alchemie	97
Café Bazar	99
Mozartsteg Pedestrian Bridge	102
Gwandhaus	104
Linzer Gasse	107
Dreifaltigkeitskirche (Holy Trinity Church)	109
MUSEUMS	112
Museum der Moderne Salzburg (Museum of Modern Art)	112
Salzburg Museum	114
Mozart's Birthplace (Mozarts Geburtshaus)	117
Mozart's Residence (Mozarts Wohnhaus)	119
Salzburg Cathedral Museum (Dommuseum Salzburg)	122
Toy Museum (Spielzeugmuseum)	124
Panorama Museum Salzburg	127
Salzburg Baroque Museum	130

St. Peter's Abbey Museum (Stift St. Peter)	132
SCULPTURES, STATUES AND MONUMENTS	135
Residenz Fountain (Residenzbrunnen)	135
Pegasus Fountain (Pegasusbrunnen)	136
Sebastian Staircase Sculptures	138
Kapitelschwemme	139
Mozart Monument	142
Monument to Hans Makart	145
University Square Statue (Universitätsplatz)	147
Glockenspiel	149
Cloak of Conscience	151
Marian Column in Salzburg	152
MUSIC AND CULTURE	155
Mozart's Legacy	155
Salzburg Festival	158
Salzburg Marionette Theater	161
Classical Music Scene	164
Traditional Folk Music	166
Architecture and History	168
Museums and Galleries	171
Cultural Events and Festivals	174
Salzburg's Cultural Heritage Sites	176
CUISINE AND CULINARY DELIGHTS	179

Salzburg Cuisine	179
Coffeehouse Culture	181
Best Restaurants	184
NATURE ESCAPES	187
Salzburg's Lakes	187
Salzburg Mountains and Hills	189
Parks and Gardens	192
Almkanal	195
Salzach River	196
Rivers	196
Gorges	198
Waterfalls	201
Kitzsteinhorn Glacier	204
TRAVEL TIPS	206
Safety Tips	206
Local Insights	208
Budget-Friendly Travel Tips	209
Solo Travel Tips in Salzburg	210
ITINERARIES	213
Mozart Heritage Tour	213
Salzburg Old Town Walking Tour	213
Sound of Music Tour	213
Nature and Hiking Expedition	214

Salzburg by Night	214
Baroque and Art Lover's Delight	214
Family Fun Day	215
Salzburg Culinary Experience	215
Musical Journey through Salzburg	215
Day Trip to the Lakes and Mountains	216
MAPS	217
Austria Map	217
Salzburg City Map	218
Salzburg Walking Tour Map	219
Sound of Music Movie Locations Map	220
Salzburg Food Market Map	221
Salzburg Accommodation Map	222
CONCLUSION	223
INDEX	224

INTRODUCTION

Welcome to Salzburg, the enchanting city that captivates visitors with its timeless charm and rich cultural heritage. Nestled in the heart of Austria, Salzburg is a destination steeped in history, art, and music, and is renowned as the birthplace of the prodigious composer, Wolfgang Amadeus Mozart. From its majestic castles and baroque architecture to its breathtaking alpine landscapes,

Salzburg offers a captivating blend of old-world elegance and natural beauty.

As you embark on your journey through Mozart's hometown, prepare to be spellbound by its atmospheric streets, picturesque riverbanks, and cultural treasures. This comprehensive travel guide will lead you through the must-visit attractions, hidden gems, and cultural experiences that make Salzburg an unparalleled destination for travelers seeking a quintessential European adventure.

Let the melodies of Mozart's music and the beauty of Salzburg's landscapes transport you to a world of elegance, history, and artistic brilliance. Discover the best of Salzburg as we unravel the city's secrets, showcase its vibrant festivals, and guide you through the warm hospitality of its residents. Your Salzburg experience awaits!

THE HISTORY OF SALZBURG

The history of Salzburg, Austria, is rich and dates back to ancient times. Here is an overview of its key historical periods:

Prehistory and Ancient Times

The area around Salzburg has been inhabited since the Neolithic period, with evidence of settlements dating back to around 5000 BC. The Celts settled in the region during the

Iron Age, and the town of Salzburg itself was founded by the Romans in the late 1st century AD, who named it "Juvavum."

Early Middle Ages

After the fall of the Roman Empire, the region came under the control of various Germanic tribes. In the 8th century, Saint Rupert, a missionary, arrived in the area and Christianized the region. He became the first Bishop of Salzburg, and the city developed as an important religious center.

Salzburg as an Independent Principality

In the 13th century, Salzburg became an independent principality ruled by powerful archbishops. These archbishops were not only religious leaders but also political figures who expanded the city's influence and power in the region.

Reformation and Counter-Reformation

In the 16th century, the Reformation movement led to religious tensions in Salzburg. However, the Counter-Reformation initiated by the Catholic Church resulted in the suppression of Protestantism in the city and reaffirmed the city's loyalty to the Catholic Church.

18th Century and Mozart

The 18th century was a golden age for Salzburg. The city became known for its Baroque architecture, and its most famous resident, Wolfgang Amadeus Mozart, was born in Salzburg in 1756. Mozart's early years were spent in the city, where he developed his musical talent.

Napoleon's Influence

In the early 19th century, Napoleon's forces occupied Salzburg, and the city came under the rule of the Austrian Empire. During this period, Salzburg's political and economic significance declined.

20th Century and World War II

In the 20th century, Salzburg faced challenges during World War II, including bombings and destruction. After the war, the city underwent a process of rebuilding and revitalization.

2023 and Beyond

Today, Salzburg is a vibrant city known for its cultural heritage, music festivals, and architectural beauty. Its historic center, with its Baroque buildings and landmarks, is a UNESCO World Heritage Site. The Salzburg Festival, founded in 1920, is one of the most renowned music and performing arts festivals in the world.

TRAVEL PRACTICALITIES

Visa and Travel Documents for Austria

Before planning your trip to Salzburg or any other part of Austria, it is essential to check the visa requirements and necessary travel documents. Here are some key points to consider:

Schengen Area:

Austria is part of the Schengen Area, which allows for border-free travel between its member countries. If you are a citizen of a Schengen Area country, you can travel to Austria without a visa for short stays.

Visa Exemptions:

Citizens of certain countries are exempt from obtaining a visa for short stays (up to 90 days) in Austria. These countries include the United States, Canada, Australia, New Zealand, Japan, and many European countries. However, it's essential to check the latest list of visa-exempt countries as it may change over time.

Visa Requirements:

If you are a citizen of a country that is not visa-exempt, you will need to apply for a Schengen visa to travel to Austria. Schengen visas allow you to travel to multiple Schengen countries during your stay.

Visa Application Process:

To apply for a Schengen visa, you will need to contact the Austrian consulate or embassy in your country. The application process usually involves submitting required documents, such as a passport, passport-sized photos, travel itinerary, proof of accommodation, travel insurance, and proof of financial means to cover your stay.

Duration of Stay:

Schengen visas typically allow for short stays of up to 90 days within a 180-day period. If you plan to stay in Austria for longer than 90 days or for purposes other than tourism, you may need to apply for a different type of visa.

Passport Validity:

Ensure that your passport is valid for at least three months beyond your planned departure date from Austria.

Travel Insurance:

It is advisable to have valid travel insurance that covers medical emergencies and repatriation during your stay in Austria.

Specific Travel Requirements:

Depending on your nationality and travel plans, there may be specific requirements or additional documents needed for your visa application.

Best Time to Visit Salzburg

The best time to visit Salzburg depends on your preferences for weather, events, and crowd levels. Salzburg offers unique experiences throughout the year, so consider the following factors to determine your ideal time to visit:

Spring (March to May):

Spring in Salzburg brings mild temperatures, blooming flowers, and longer days. It's a fantastic time to explore the city's gardens, parks, and historic sites without the peak tourist crowds. Easter festivities and concerts also add to the charm of the season.

Summer (June to August):

Summer is the peak tourist season in Salzburg, thanks to warm temperatures and a full calendar of festivals and events. The Salzburg Festival, with world-class music and theater performances, takes place in July and August, making it an ideal time for arts enthusiasts.

Autumn (September to November):

Autumn brings a beautiful display of fall foliage to Salzburg, creating picturesque scenes across the city. The weather remains pleasant, and there are fewer crowds compared to summer. It's a great time for scenic walks and exploring the surrounding countryside.

Winter (December to February):

Winter transforms Salzburg into a fairytale winter wonderland, especially during the Christmas season. The city's famous Christmas markets offer a magical atmosphere with festive decorations, concerts, and traditional Austrian treats. If you enjoy winter sports, nearby ski resorts offer excellent opportunities for skiing and snowboarding.

Christmas Markets (Late November to December):

If you're a fan of Christmas markets, visiting Salzburg during the Advent season is a must. The city's markets, including the Christkindlmarkt at Residenzplatz and the Christmas market at Hellbrunn Palace, are among the most enchanting in Europe.

Off-Peak Travel (Late Winter to Early Spring and Late Autumn):

Late winter and early spring, as well as late autumn, offer more affordable accommodation rates and fewer tourists. While the weather may be cooler, you can still enjoy indoor attractions and the city's cultural offerings.

How to Get to Salzburg

Getting to Salzburg is convenient as the city is well-connected by various modes of transportation. Here are the primary ways to reach Salzburg:

By Air:

Salzburg Airport W.A. Mozart (SZG) is the city's main international airport, located just 4 kilometers (2.5 miles) from the city center. It serves both domestic and international flights, making it a convenient choice for travelers arriving from different parts of the world.

By Train:

Salzburg is well-connected to major cities across Europe by train. The main train station, Salzburg Hauptbahnhof, is centrally located and offers direct connections to cities like Vienna, Munich, Innsbruck, Zurich, and others. Train travel is a comfortable and scenic option, especially for travelers coming from nearby countries.

By Car:

Traveling to Salzburg by car is a popular option, especially for visitors coming from neighboring countries. The city is easily accessible via major highways, and driving through the picturesque landscapes of Austria is a delightful experience.

By Bus:

Several long-distance bus companies operate services to Salzburg from various European cities. The bus station is located near the main train station, making it convenient for travelers arriving by bus.

By Bike:

For more adventurous travelers, biking to Salzburg is also an option. The city is well-connected to nearby cycling routes, and bike rentals are available for exploring the region's scenic countryside.

From Vienna:

Traveling from Vienna to Salzburg is easy and fast by train, with frequent connections and a journey time of around 2.5 to 3 hours. High-speed trains, such as Railjet, operate between the two cities.

From Munich:

Munich is another major gateway to Salzburg. Trains run regularly between Munich and Salzburg, with a journey time of approximately 1.5 to 2 hours.

From Innsbruck:

Travelers coming from Innsbruck can also take direct trains to Salzburg, with a journey time of around 1.5 to 2.5 hours, depending on the train type.

Getting Around Salzburg

Getting around Salzburg is convenient and easy, thanks to its efficient public transportation system and pedestrian-friendly layout. Here are the primary modes of transportation in Salzburg:

Walking:

Salzburg's historic city center is compact and best explored on foot. Many of the city's main attractions, such as Mirabell Palace, Mozart's Birthplace, and Salzburg Cathedral, are within walking distance of each other.

Public Transportation:

Salzburg has an excellent public transportation network that includes buses and trams. The Salzburger Verkehrsverbund (SVV) manages the city's public transport system, and tickets are valid for both buses and trams. Public transportation is a convenient way to reach destinations outside the city center and explore the surrounding areas.

Salzburg Card:

For visitors planning to use public transportation extensively and visit multiple attractions, the Salzburg Card is a cost-effective option. The card provides free access to city buses and trams, as well as free or discounted entry to various museums and attractions.

Bicycles:

Cycling is a popular mode of transportation in Salzburg, and the city has well-maintained cycling paths and bike rental services. Renting a bike allows you to explore the city and its surroundings at your own pace.

Taxis and Rideshares:

Taxis are readily available throughout the city, and rideshare services like Uber operate in Salzburg as well. Taxis are a convenient option for traveling to specific locations or getting to and from the airport.

Tourist Train:

For a fun and informative way to see the city, consider taking a ride on the Salzburg tourist train. The train offers guided tours around the city's major sights, providing an overview of Salzburg's history and attractions.

Salzach River Cruise:

A river cruise along the Salzach River is a scenic and relaxing way to see the city from a different perspective. Several companies offer boat tours, allowing you to admire Salzburg's skyline and architecture from the water.

Horse-Drawn Carriages:

For a romantic and nostalgic experience, take a horse-drawn carriage ride through Salzburg's streets. Carriages are available for hire near major tourist spots like Mirabell Gardens and Residenzplatz.

Accommodation in Salzburg

Salzburg offers a wide range of accommodation options to suit every traveler's preferences and budget. From luxury hotels to cozy guesthouses and budget-friendly hostels, the city has something for everyone. Here are the primary types of accommodation in Salzburg:

Hotels:

Salzburg boasts numerous hotels, ranging from 5-star luxury establishments to charming boutique hotels. Many hotels are located in the city center, making it convenient to explore the main attractions on foot. Amenities typically include restaurants, bars, fitness centers, and concierge services.

Guesthouses and Bed and Breakfasts:

Guesthouses and bed and breakfasts offer a more intimate and personalized experience. These accommodations are often family-run and provide a cozy atmosphere, along with home-cooked breakfasts.

Hostels and Budget Accommodations:

For budget-conscious travelers and backpackers, hostels and budget accommodations are plentiful in Salzburg. These options offer shared dormitory rooms or private rooms at affordable rates, making them ideal for solo travelers or groups.

Apartments and Vacation Rentals:

If you prefer a home-away-from-home experience, consider renting an apartment or vacation home in Salzburg. This option is perfect for families or travelers who want the convenience of a kitchen and extra space.

Boutique Hotels:

Boutique hotels in Salzburg offer a unique and stylish ambiance, often with personalized service and attention to detail. These properties are ideal for travelers seeking a more exclusive and intimate stay.

Luxury Resorts:

For those looking for a lavish and indulgent experience, Salzburg has several luxury resorts and spa hotels set in picturesque locations, providing a tranquil retreat from the city's hustle and bustle.

Hostels with Social Events:

Some hostels in Salzburg organize social events, pub crawls, and city tours, making them ideal for solo travelers or those looking to meet new people and explore the city together.

Hotels with Views:

Several hotels in Salzburg offer stunning views of the city's landmarks, such as Hohensalzburg Fortress or the Salzach River, adding an extra touch of magic to your stay.

Shopping in Salzburg

Shopping in Salzburg offers a delightful blend of traditional crafts, local specialties, high-end fashion, and unique souvenirs. The city's charming streets are lined with boutique shops, specialty stores, and bustling markets, providing a diverse shopping experience for visitors. Here are some of the best shopping spots in Salzburg:

Getreidegasse:

Getreidegasse is Salzburg's most famous shopping street, known for its narrow medieval alleyways and traditional storefronts. Here, you'll find a mix of upscale boutiques, international fashion brands, and shops selling local crafts and souvenirs.

Linzergasse:

Linzergasse is another picturesque shopping street with a historic ambiance. It offers a variety of shops selling clothing, accessories, antiques, and Austrian delicacies.

Mozartkugel Shops:

Mozartkugel is a famous local specialty, and you'll find shops dedicated to selling these delicious chocolate and marzipan treats all over the city. Look for the original "Fürst" brand for the authentic Mozartkugel experience.

Salzburg Christmas Markets:

During the Advent season, Salzburg's Christmas markets offer a magical shopping experience. The Christkindlmarkt at Residenzplatz and the Christmas market at Hellbrunn Palace are among the most popular.

Traditional Crafts:

Salzburg is known for its traditional crafts, including handmade clothing, leather goods, glassware, and wooden carvings. Shop for these unique crafts at stores like "Steindl Trachten" for traditional Austrian clothing and "Richter Mandl" for handcrafted wooden products.

Mirabellplatz Market:

On Thursdays, the Mirabellplatz hosts a vibrant farmers' market, where you can find fresh produce, local cheeses, baked goods, and more.

Goldgasse and Judengasse:

These charming streets are home to boutique shops and art galleries, perfect for browsing unique finds and artistic treasures.

Designer Outlets:

For discounted designer brands, head to Designer Outlet Salzburg, located a short distance from the city center.

Bookstores and Antique Shops:

Book lovers will enjoy exploring Salzburg's bookstores, some of which sell antique and rare books. "Antiquariat Bücherschmaus" is one such store that specializes in antiquarian books.

Salzburger Schatzkammer:

For exquisite jewelry and gemstones, visit Salzburger Schatzkammer, a store offering beautiful pieces inspired by the city's history and culture.

Health and Safety

Health and safety are essential considerations for any traveler visiting Salzburg or any other destination. Here are some important tips to ensure a safe and healthy trip:

Travel Insurance:

Before traveling to Salzburg, make sure you have comprehensive travel insurance that covers medical emergencies, trip cancellations, and other unforeseen events.

Vaccinations and Health Precautions:

Check with your healthcare provider or travel clinic to ensure that you are up-to-date on routine vaccinations and to inquire about any additional vaccinations or health precautions recommended for Austria.

Stay Hydrated:

Especially during warm weather or physical activities, stay hydrated by drinking plenty of water.

Sun Protection:

During sunny days, protect yourself from the sun by wearing sunscreen, sunglasses, and a hat.

Dress Appropriately:

Salzburg experiences different weather conditions throughout the year, so pack appropriate clothing to stay comfortable and prepared for the climate during your visit.

Food and Water Safety:

Tap water in Salzburg is safe to drink, but if you prefer bottled water, it is readily available. Ensure that the food you consume is from reputable sources and properly cooked.

Safety in Public Spaces:

Salzburg is generally a safe city, but like any other place, be mindful of your belongings and surroundings in public spaces to avoid petty theft.

Emergency Numbers:

Familiarize yourself with emergency contact numbers in Salzburg, including local police, medical, and fire services.

COVID-19 Guidelines:

Check the latest COVID-19 guidelines and travel restrictions for Austria before your trip, and adhere to any local health and safety protocols during your stay.

Medications and Prescriptions:

Bring an adequate supply of any necessary medications, along with a copy of your prescriptions, in case you need medical attention during your trip.

Be Cautious with Strangers:

While Salzburg is generally safe, exercise caution when interacting with strangers and be wary of potential scams or pickpocketing in crowded areas.

Follow Local Laws and Customs:

Respect local customs and laws in Salzburg to avoid any legal issues or cultural misunderstandings.

Emergency Medical Services:

Familiarize yourself with the location of hospitals and medical facilities in Salzburg in case of any medical emergencies.

Safe Transportation:

Use reputable transportation services and follow safety guidelines while using public transport or hiring taxis.

Currency and Payments

The currency used in Salzburg and throughout Austria is the Euro (€). As a member of the Eurozone, Austria adopted the Euro as its official currency in 2002, replacing the Austrian Schilling. Here are some important points about currency and payments in Salzburg:

Currency Denominations:

The Euro is divided into coins (cents) and banknotes. Coins come in denominations of 1, 2, 5, 10, 20, and 50 cents, as well as 1 and 2 Euros. Banknotes are available in denominations of 5, 10, 20, 50, 100, 200, and 500 Euros.

Accepted Payment Methods:

Cash is widely accepted in Salzburg, especially for smaller purchases and in traditional establishments. However, major credit and debit cards (Visa, Mastercard, and sometimes

American Express) are accepted at most hotels, restaurants, shops, and tourist attractions.

ATM Availability:

ATMs (Automated Teller Machines) are readily available throughout Salzburg, allowing you to withdraw Euros using your debit or credit card. They are typically found near banks, shopping areas, and major tourist spots.

Currency Exchange:

Currency exchange services are available at banks, exchange offices, and some hotels in Salzburg. Banks usually offer competitive exchange rates, but it's a good idea to compare rates and fees before exchanging money.

Tipping:

Tipping is not obligatory in Austria, but it is customary to leave a small tip if you are satisfied with the service. In restaurants, rounding up the bill or leaving an additional 5-10% is common.

Tax-Free Shopping:

Non-European Union residents are eligible for tax-free shopping in Austria. Look for stores displaying the "Tax-Free Shopping" sign and inquire about the process for claiming your VAT (Value Added Tax) refund.

Contactless Payments:

Contactless payments, using cards or mobile payment apps, are widely accepted in many establishments in Salzburg.

Currency Exchange at the Airport:

If you need to exchange currency upon arrival, keep in mind that airport exchange offices may offer less favorable rates compared to those in the city center.

Travel Insurance

Travel insurance is a type of insurance that provides coverage and protection for travelers in case of unexpected events or emergencies that may occur during their trip. It is designed to offer financial assistance and support in situations such as trip cancellations, medical emergencies, lost or delayed baggage, flight delays, and other travel-related issues. Travel insurance plans offer various types of coverage, and the level of coverage may vary depending on the policy you choose. Common coverage options include:

- Trip Cancellation/Interruption
- Medical Expenses
- Reimbursement for lost, stolen, or damaged baggage and personal items during your trip.
- Travel Delay
- Emergency Assistance

Packing Essentials

When packing for your trip to Salzburg, it's essential to bring the right items to ensure a comfortable and enjoyable journey. Here is a list of packing essentials to consider:

Clothing:

- Weather-appropriate clothing
- Comfortable walking shoes
- Raincoat or umbrella

Travel Documents:

- Passport and visa (if required)
- Travel insurance documents
- Flight tickets and accommodation confirmations.
- **Personal Items:**
- Prescription medications and necessary health supplies.
- Toiletries
- Sunscreen and sunglasses for sunny days.

Electronics:

- Camera or smartphone for capturing memorable moments.

- ❖ Travel adapter: Salzburg uses Type C and Type F electrical outlets.

- ❖ Portable charger for your devices.

Money and Security:

- ❖ Euros (local currency) and a secure travel wallet.

- ❖ Credit/debit cards

- ❖ Copy of important documents

Guidebooks and Maps:

- ❖ A guidebook or digital travel guide with information about Salzburg's attractions, restaurants, and local customs.

- ❖ A map of Salzburg's city center to help you navigate the streets.

Reusable Water Bottle:

- ❖ Stay hydrated while exploring the city by carrying a reusable water bottle.

Daypack or Backpack:

- ❖ A small daypack or backpack for carrying your essentials during daily outings.

Medications and First Aid Kit:

- ❖ Include any necessary medications and a basic first aid kit with band-aids, antiseptic, and pain relievers.

Comfort Items:

❖ Earplugs and a sleep mask for better rest during your travels.

Comfortable Travel Clothes:

❖ Comfortable clothes for long flights or train rides.

Language

The official language of Salzburg, and Austria as a whole, is German. German is spoken by the majority of the population, and all official documents, signs, and communication are in German. As a tourist destination, many people in Salzburg, especially those in the tourism industry, speak English to some extent, particularly in hotels, restaurants, and tourist attractions. English is commonly understood and used, especially in the city center and at popular tourist sites.

While English is widely spoken, it is always appreciated when visitors make an effort to learn a few basic German phrases and greetings. Locals generally respond positively to tourists attempting to speak the local language, even if it's just a simple "Hallo" (Hello) or "Danke" (Thank you).

If you plan to venture outside the main tourist areas or explore the Austrian countryside, especially in rural areas, knowledge of some basic German phrases can be helpful as English proficiency may be less common. However, don't worry too much about language barriers, as Salzburg is a welcoming city for international visitors, and people are generally helpful and accommodating to tourists from all over the world.

Electrical Outlets

In Salzburg, Austria, the electrical outlets are of the Type C and Type F standard. Here are the details about these electrical outlets:

Type C Outlets:

Type C outlets are the standard European two-pin plugs. They have two round pins and are commonly used in Austria. The voltage used in Austria is 230V, and the frequency is 50Hz.

Type F Outlets:

Type F outlets, also known as Schuko or "grounded" outlets, are also widely used in Austria. They have two round pins like Type C outlets but also have two additional grounding clips on the sides. Type F outlets are compatible with Type C plugs.

Emergency Numbers

In Austria, including Salzburg, the emergency numbers for various emergency services are as follows:

- ❖ Medical Emergency / Ambulance: 144
- ❖ Fire Brigade: 122
- ❖ Police: 133

❖ European Emergency Number: 112

Local Customs and Etiquette

When visiting Salzburg, it is important to be aware of local customs and etiquette to ensure a respectful and enjoyable experience. Here are some key customs and etiquette practices to keep in mind:

Greetings:

When meeting someone for the first time, it is customary to offer a handshake and address them with "Guten Tag" (Good day). In more informal settings, a simple "Hallo" (Hello) is also appropriate.

Titles and Formality:

Austrians value formalities, especially when addressing strangers or elders. Use "Herr" (Mr.) or "Frau" (Mrs./Ms.) followed by the person's last name when speaking to them for the first time. If they offer their first name during the conversation, it is acceptable to use it.

Punctuality:

Austrians appreciate punctuality. If you have an appointment or reservation, try to arrive on time or a few minutes early.

Table Manners:

When dining in restaurants or at someone's home, wait for the host to say "Guten Appetit" (Enjoy your meal) before beginning to eat. Keep your hands visible on the table, and refrain from resting your elbows on it.

Tipping:

Tipping is customary in Austria, but it is not mandatory. A gratuity of 5-10% of the bill is considered polite and appreciated, especially in restaurants and for good service.

Smoking Regulations:

Austria has strict smoking regulations, and smoking is generally not allowed in public indoor spaces, including restaurants, cafes, and public transport.

Quiet and Respectful Behavior:

Austrians appreciate quiet and respectful behavior, especially in public places like museums, churches, and public transport.

Dress Code:

Salzburg is a relatively formal city, and dressing neatly and modestly is appreciated, especially when visiting religious sites.

Photography Etiquette:

Always ask for permission before taking photos of people, particularly in more intimate or personal settings.

Language:

While many people in Salzburg speak English, learning a few basic German phrases can be a polite gesture and may come in handy in certain situations.

Internet and Communication

Internet and communication services in Salzburg are well-developed and widely available, making it easy for travelers to stay connected during their visit. Here are some key points about internet and communication in Salzburg:

Internet Access:

Most hotels, cafes, restaurants, and tourist attractions in Salzburg offer free Wi-Fi for guests. Many public spaces, such as parks and plazas, also provide free Wi-Fi. You can easily connect to these networks with your smartphone, tablet, or laptop.

Mobile Data:

If you prefer mobile data for internet access, you can purchase a local SIM card from one of the major mobile network providers in Austria. This will give you access to mobile data and allow you to use your smartphone for internet browsing, navigation, and communication throughout your trip.

Communication Apps:

Popular communication apps such as WhatsApp, Facebook Messenger, and Skype are commonly used in Salzburg for messaging and making voice and video calls. Using these apps over Wi-Fi can be a cost-effective way to stay in touch with family and friends back home.

Roaming Charges:

If you plan to use your mobile phone with your home SIM card, be aware of roaming charges, as these can be expensive. Check with your mobile provider about international roaming packages before traveling to Salzburg to avoid unexpected charges.

Phone Booths:

Public phone booths are still available in some locations in Salzburg, but they are becoming less common due to the widespread use of mobile phones. Phone cards are usually required to use public phone booths.

ACTIVITIES

Salzburg offers a wide range of activities to suit different interests and preferences. Whether you're interested in history, music, nature, or culinary delights, there's something for everyone to enjoy in this beautiful city. Here are some popular activities in Salzburg:

Boat Rides

Boat rides in Salzburg offer a unique and scenic way to experience the city and its surroundings from the water. Here are some popular boat rides and tours in Salzburg:

Salzach River Cruise:

Take a leisurely cruise along the Salzach River, passing by iconic landmarks such as Hohensalzburg Fortress, Mirabell Palace, and Mozart's Birthplace.

Amadeus Salzburg River Cruise:

Enjoy a relaxing cruise on the Amadeus Salzburg, a comfortable boat with indoor and outdoor seating, offering panoramic views of the city.

Evening Panorama Cruise:

Experience the magic of Salzburg at night with an evening panorama cruise, admiring the city's illuminated skyline and landmarks.

Sound of Music Tour by Boat:

Combine a boat ride with a "Sound of Music" tour, sailing along the Salzach River while passing film locations from the famous movie.

Hellbrunn Palace Boat Ride:

Visit Hellbrunn Palace and take a boat ride on the palace's scenic pond, passing by trick fountains and historic pavilions.

River Taxi:

Use a river taxi service to hop on and off at different points along the Salzach River, providing a convenient and flexible mode of transportation.

Lake Wolfgang Cruise:

Take a day trip to Lake Wolfgang (Wolfgangsee) and enjoy a relaxing boat cruise on the crystal-clear waters surrounded by stunning mountain scenery.

River Adventure Tours:

Join guided river adventure tours, such as paddleboarding or kayaking, to explore the Salzach River from a more active perspective.

Boat and Bike Combination Tours:

Combine a boat ride with a cycling tour, offering a delightful way to explore both the city and the countryside.

Seasonal Themed Cruises:

Look out for seasonal themed cruises, such as Christmas markets cruises during the Advent season, offering a festive and unique experience.

Take a Day Trip

Taking a day trip from Salzburg allows you to explore the beautiful surroundings and nearby attractions. Here are some wonderful day trip options from Salzburg:

Hallstatt:

Visit the picturesque town of Hallstatt, a UNESCO World Heritage site, known for its stunning alpine setting and charming lakeside houses.

Berchtesgaden and Eagle's Nest:

Explore the Berchtesgaden National Park and take a bus tour to the historic Eagle's Nest, offering breathtaking views of the Bavarian Alps.

Lake Wolfgang (Wolfgangsee):

Take a boat trip on Lake Wolfgang, visit the charming towns of St. Wolfgang and St. Gilgen, and enjoy the scenic beauty of the Salzkammergut region.

Werfen and Eisriesenwelt Ice Caves:

Visit Werfen and explore the Eisriesenwelt Ice Caves, the largest ice caves in the world, nestled within the stunning Tennengebirge Mountains.

Salzkammergut Lakes and Villages:

Discover the enchanting landscapes of the Salzkammergut region, visiting beautiful lakes and traditional Austrian villages like St. Gilgen and Mondsee.

Innsbruck:

Take a train or bus to the charming city of Innsbruck, surrounded by the majestic peaks of the Austrian Alps.

Salzburg Lake District:

Explore the Salzburg Lake District, including the Fuschlsee and Mondsee, for serene lakes and charming villages.

Königssee and Ramsau Church:

Journey to Königssee, a stunning lake known for its crystal-clear waters, and visit the charming Ramsau Church with the Watzmann Mountain as a backdrop.

Salzburg Salt Mines (Salzwelten):

Take a tour of the Salzburg Salt Mines in Hallein or Berchtesgaden for an exciting underground adventure.

Bavarian Mountains and Chiemsee:

Venture into Bavaria to explore the Bavarian Alps and visit the Chiemsee, also known as the "Bavarian Sea," with its beautiful island palaces.

Outdoor Activities

Salzburg offers a variety of exciting outdoor activities, perfect for nature enthusiasts and adventure seekers. Here are some popular outdoor activities to enjoy in and around Salzburg:

Cycling:

Rent a bike and cycle along the Salzach River or explore the countryside on scenic cycling routes.

Stand-Up Paddleboarding (SUP):

Try stand-up paddleboarding on the Salzach River for a fun and active water adventure.

Rock Climbing:

Enjoy rock climbing in the nearby Berchtesgaden National Park or on the Klettersteig routes in the surrounding mountains.

Paragliding:

Experience the thrill of paragliding over the beautiful landscapes of Salzburg with trained instructors.

Horseback Riding:

Take a horseback riding tour through the countryside or in the picturesque Salzkammergut region.

White-Water Rafting:

Venture out on a white-water rafting excursion on the Salzach River for an adrenaline-pumping experience.

Canyoning:

Embark on a canyoning adventure, exploring the region's gorges, waterfalls, and natural pools.

Zip-Lining:

Experience the thrill of zip-lining across the mountains and forests in nearby adventure parks.

Golfing:

Play a round of golf at one of Salzburg's golf courses, surrounded by scenic landscapes.

Picnicking:

Enjoy a relaxing picnic in one of Salzburg's beautiful parks, such as Mirabell Gardens or Stadtpark.

Outdoor Swimming:

Take a dip in one of Salzburg's outdoor pools or head to Lake Wolfgang (Wolfgangsee) for a refreshing swim.

Segway Tours:

Join a guided Segway tour to explore Salzburg's landmarks and surroundings in a unique way.

Nightlife in Salzburg

Salzburg offers a vibrant and diverse nightlife scene, with something to suit every taste. While the city's nightlife may not be as lively as in larger urban centers, it still provides ample opportunities for evening entertainment and socializing. Here are some highlights of the nightlife in Salzburg:

Pubs and Beer Gardens:

Enjoy a relaxed evening at one of Salzburg's cozy pubs or traditional beer gardens, where you can savor a wide selection of local and international beers.

Jazz Clubs and Live Music Venues:

Experience the city's musical heritage by visiting jazz clubs and live music venues, where you can enjoy performances by talented local musicians and bands.

Classical Concerts:

Salzburg, known as the "City of Mozart," offers a variety of classical music concerts, including performances at historic venues like the Salzburg State Theatre and the Mozarteum.

Casino Salzburg:

Test your luck and enjoy a night of gaming at Casino Salzburg, situated in a beautiful palace setting.

Late-Night Cafés:

Relax and unwind at one of Salzburg's late-night cafés, offering a cozy ambiance and delicious coffee and desserts.

Nightclubs and Bars:

Dance the night away at one of Salzburg's nightclubs and bars, which often host themed parties and events.

Salzach River Cruise:

Experience a unique nighttime perspective of Salzburg's illuminated skyline with a romantic Salzach River cruise.

Adventurous Night Tours:

Join adventurous night tours, such as ghost tours or night walks, to learn about the city's legends and spooky stories.

Summer Festivals and Events:

During the summer, the city hosts various festivals and open-air events, providing a lively atmosphere and entertainment.

Salzburg's Festive Advent Season:

During the Advent season, Salzburg's Christmas markets and festive events create a magical and festive ambiance.

Irish and English Pubs:

Enjoy the international atmosphere of Salzburg's Irish and English pubs, where you can find a mix of locals and travelers.

Family-Friendly Activities

Salzburg is a fantastic destination for families, offering a wide range of family-friendly activities that cater to all ages. Here are some fun and family-friendly activities to enjoy in Salzburg:

Salzburg Zoo (Tiergarten Hellbrunn):

Visit the Salzburg Zoo to see over 140 animal species, including lions, elephants, and penguins.

Mirabell Gardens and Playground:

Explore the beautiful Mirabell Gardens, where kids can enjoy the playground and run around in open green spaces.

Hohensalzburg Fortress:

Take the funicular to Hohensalzburg Fortress, where kids can explore the castle grounds and enjoy interactive exhibits.

Haus der Natur (House of Nature):

Discover the interactive exhibits and hands-on activities at Haus der Natur, a fascinating museum for kids of all ages.

Salzach River Cruise:

Enjoy a family-friendly boat ride on the Salzach River, offering scenic views of the city and its landmarks.

Hellbrunn Palace and Trick Fountains:

Visit Hellbrunn Palace to explore the beautiful gardens and experience the surprise of the trick fountains.

Toy Museum (Spielzeugmuseum):

Step into a world of toys and nostalgia at the Toy Museum, featuring an extensive collection of historic toys.

Salzach Park and Kapuzinerberg Hill:

Take a leisurely walk through Salzach Park or embark on a family hike up Kapuzinerberg Hill for beautiful views.

Boat Rental on Lake Wolfgang (Wolfgangsee):

Enjoy a family boat ride on Lake Wolfgang, rent a pedal boat, or take a scenic boat tour on the lake.

Advent Markets during Christmas:

Experience the magical atmosphere of Salzburg's Christmas markets during the Advent season, where kids can enjoy festive activities and treats.

Family-Friendly Cafés and Restaurants:

Explore the family-friendly cafés and restaurants in Salzburg, offering children's menus and play areas.

Salzburg Museum:

Visit the Salzburg Museum for engaging exhibits and activities suitable for young visitors.

Visit Christmas Markets

Visiting the Christmas markets in Salzburg is a magical and enchanting experience, especially during the Advent season. The city comes alive with festive decorations, twinkling lights, and the sweet aroma of mulled wine and roasted chestnuts. Here are some must-visit Christmas markets in Salzburg:

Christkindlmarkt at Domplatz (Cathedral Square):

The Christkindlmarkt at Domplatz is the largest and most famous Christmas market in Salzburg. It is located in front of the Salzburg Cathedral and features over 100 beautifully decorated stalls offering crafts, gifts, and seasonal treats.

Hellbrunn Palace Advent Market:

The Hellbrunn Palace Advent Market is located in the beautiful palace courtyard and gardens. It offers a festive ambiance with stalls selling handmade crafts and local delicacies.

St. Leonhard Advent Market:

The St. Leonhard Advent Market is known for its charming and cozy atmosphere. It is situated in the courtyard of St. Leonhard Church and features artisanal products and traditional Austrian treats.

Mirabell Palace Christmas Market:

The Mirabell Palace Christmas Market is set against the stunning backdrop of Mirabell Palace and gardens. It offers a delightful selection of handicrafts, decorations, and culinary delights.

Stern Advent Market on the Kapitelplatz:

The Stern Advent Market on the Kapitelplatz is known for its unique "Stern Tower," where visitors can climb for panoramic views of Salzburg. The market also features artisanal products and culinary delights.

Advent Market at the Hohensalzburg Fortress:

The Advent Market at Hohensalzburg Fortress offers a festive experience within the historic walls of the fortress. Enjoy crafts, food, and stunning views of the city.

Silent Night Advent Market at Stille Nacht Kapelle (Silent Night Chapel) in Oberndorf:

This special market is held at the location where the world-famous Christmas carol "Silent Night" was first performed. It's a short trip from Salzburg and offers a nostalgic and authentic Christmas experience.

Wolfgangsee Advent Market:

Take a day trip to the nearby Wolfgangsee and enjoy its charming Advent market set against the backdrop of the beautiful lake.

Shopping

Salzburg offers a delightful shopping experience with a mix of traditional markets, boutique stores, and well-known brands. Here are some of the best shopping areas and places to shop in Salzburg:

Getreidegasse:

This historic shopping street is one of the city's most famous, lined with charming old buildings and traditional shopfronts. Here, you can find a mix of international brands, local boutiques, and souvenir shops.

Linzer Gasse:

Another popular shopping street in Salzburg, Linzer Gasse is known for its diverse range of shops, including clothing stores, art galleries, and unique shops selling handmade crafts.

Salzburg Food Market (Schranne):

For a taste of local flavors, visit the Salzburg Food Market, where you can shop for fresh produce, local delicacies, and regional specialties.

Salzburg Old Market (Altstadt Market):

Held every Thursday, the Old Market offers a range of stalls selling clothing, accessories, crafts, and food products.

Europark Salzburg:

This modern shopping center is located just outside the city center and features over 130 shops, including fashion, electronics, and home goods stores.

Designer Outlets Salzburg:

If you're looking for designer brands at discounted prices, head to the Designer Outlets Salzburg, offering high-end fashion at affordable prices.

Mozart Souvenirs:

Don't miss the opportunity to buy souvenirs related to Mozart, such as music CDs, books, and Mozart chocolates, as a reminder of your visit to the "City of Mozart."

Christmas Markets:

During the Advent season, Salzburg's Christmas markets are a perfect place to shop for unique gifts, handmade crafts, and Christmas decorations.

Artisanal Shops:

Look out for artisanal shops and boutiques, offering handmade crafts, jewelry, and locally produced items.

Antique Shops:

If you're a fan of antiques, explore the city's antique shops for unique finds and vintage treasures.

Attend a Festive Event

Salzburg is renowned for its festive events throughout the year, but the most magical time to attend a festive event is during the Advent season leading up to Christmas. Here are some of the top festive events in Salzburg:

Salzburg Advent Singing:

Enjoy the heartwarming Salzburg Advent Singing performances, which feature traditional Austrian and Christmas songs performed by local choirs and musicians.

Silent Night Anniversary Celebration:

Visit the nearby village of Oberndorf to commemorate the creation of the world-famous Christmas carol "Silent Night." The Silent Night Chapel and celebrations are especially magical during the Advent season.

Advent Brass Music at the Hohensalzburg Fortress:

Listen to festive brass music concerts at the Hohensalzburg Fortress, where musicians play Christmas classics and joyful tunes.

Salzburg Marionette Theater:

Attend a special holiday-themed performance at the Salzburg Marionette Theater, where classic fairy tales and Christmas stories come to life through puppetry.

Advent and Christmas Concerts:

Immerse yourself in the city's musical heritage by attending Advent and Christmas concerts at iconic venues like the Salzburg Cathedral and Mozarteum.

Advent Workshops and Craft Fairs:

Participate in Advent workshops where you can learn traditional crafts like candle making and wreath decorating, or visit craft fairs to purchase handmade gifts.

Advent Market at Hellbrunn Palace:

Visit the Advent market in the courtyard of Hellbrunn Palace, where you can enjoy holiday decorations, local crafts, and delicious food.

Salzburg Advent Calendar at Residenzplatz:

Witness the lighting of the giant Advent calendar at Residenzplatz, where a new window is opened each day leading up to Christmas.

Salzburg Advent Brass at Mirabellplatz:

Listen to brass musicians playing Advent and Christmas music at Mirabellplatz, adding to the festive atmosphere.

Strolls and Hikes

Salzburg offers a range of delightful strolls and scenic hikes, allowing visitors to explore the city's historic landmarks, natural beauty, and surrounding landscapes. Here are some of the best strolls and hikes in and around Salzburg:

Old Town Stroll:

Take a leisurely stroll through Salzburg's charming Old Town (Altstadt) to explore its historic architecture, quaint streets, and iconic landmarks like the Salzburg Cathedral and Residenzplatz.

Mirabell Gardens Stroll:

Enjoy a relaxing walk through the beautiful Mirabell Gardens, known for its well-maintained flowerbeds, sculptures, and enchanting ambiance.

Kapuzinerberg Hike:

Embark on a moderate hike up Kapuzinerberg Hill for panoramic views of Salzburg, the Salzach River, and the surrounding mountains.

Mönchsberg Hill Hike:

Hike the trails on Mönchsberg Hill to reach the Museum der Moderne or the Hohensalzburg Fortress, and enjoy picturesque views of the city.

Gaisberg Mountain Hike:

For a more challenging hike, head to Gaisberg Mountain, offering rewarding views of Salzburg and the surrounding Alpine scenery.

Hellbrunn Palace Park Stroll:

Explore the beautiful gardens of Hellbrunn Palace, including the trick fountains and the Sound of Music Pavilion.

Untersberg Mountain Hike:

Take a cable car to the top of Untersberg Mountain and embark on various hiking trails to enjoy breathtaking views of Salzburg and the Austrian Alps.

Lake Fuschl Stroll:

Visit Lake Fuschl (Fuschlsee) for a relaxing stroll along its shores, surrounded by stunning landscapes.

Lake Wolfgang (Wolfgangsee) Hike:

Explore the hiking trails around Lake Wolfgang, offering captivating views of the lake and the surrounding mountains.

Stadtpark Stroll:

Take a leisurely stroll through Stadtpark, a charming city park featuring sculptures and serene green spaces.

Lake Hintersee Hike:

Venture to Lake Hintersee for a tranquil hike in a picturesque Alpine setting.

TOP ATTRACTIONS IN SALZBURG

Salzburg is a city filled with captivating attractions that showcase its rich history, culture, and natural beauty. Here are the top attractions in Salzburg that you should not miss during your visit:

Salzburg Old Town (Altstadt)

Salzburg Old Town, also known as Altstadt, is the historic heart and soul of the city. Nestled between the Salzach River and the Mönchsberg hill, it is a beautifully preserved UNESCO World Heritage Site and one of the most enchanting old towns in Europe. With its narrow cobblestone streets, ornate Baroque architecture, and charming squares, Altstadt transports visitors back in time to a bygone era of elegance and splendor. Here are some of the highlights of Salzburg Old Town:

Getreidegasse:

The iconic Getreidegasse is Salzburg's most famous shopping street, lined with historic buildings and wrought-iron signs. It is a bustling thoroughfare known for its boutiques, shops, and the birthplace of Wolfgang Amadeus Mozart.

Mozart's Birthplace:

Visit the house where the famous composer Wolfgang Amadeus Mozart was born on January 27, 1756. The museum inside showcases Mozart's life and exhibits his musical instruments, family portraits, and personal belongings.

Salzburg Residenz Palace:

The Salzburg Residenz was the former palace of the Prince-Archbishops of Salzburg. Marvel at its opulent rooms and artistic treasures, including the stunning Marble Hall.

Salzburg Cathedral (Salzburger Dom):

This majestic Baroque cathedral, dedicated to Saint Rupert and Saint Vergilius, is an architectural masterpiece with its impressive facade and domed towers. Inside, admire the magnificent organ and stunning artwork.

Residenzplatz and Residenz Gallery:

The Residenzplatz is the main square of Salzburg Old Town, surrounded by historic buildings. The Residenz Gallery houses an extensive collection of European art from the 16th to the 19th century.

Hohensalzburg Fortress:

Perched atop the Festungsberg hill, Hohensalzburg Fortress overlooks the Old Town and offers breathtaking views of the city and the surrounding Alps. Access the fortress via a funicular ride or a scenic walk.

St. Peter's Abbey and Cemetery:

St. Peter's Abbey is one of the oldest monasteries in the German-speaking world, dating back to the 7th century. The adjacent St. Peter's Cemetery is a peaceful and atmospheric burial ground.

DomQuartier Salzburg:

The DomQuartier is a unique museum complex that combines the Salzburg Cathedral, the Residenz, and the Domplatz to offer an immersive journey through Salzburg's history.

Festivals and Events:

Salzburg Old Town is a vibrant hub for cultural events and festivals throughout the year, including the Salzburg Festival, concerts, and street performances.

Horse-Drawn Carriage Rides:

Experience the charm of Salzburg Old Town with a horse-drawn carriage ride, a delightful way to explore its historic streets.

Hohensalzburg Fortress

Hohensalzburg Fortress, or Festung Hohensalzburg in German, is an iconic symbol of Salzburg's history and one of the largest fully preserved medieval fortresses in Europe. Perched on the Festungsberg hill overlooking the city, the fortress offers panoramic views of Salzburg and the stunning Alpine landscape. Here are some highlights and key features of Hohensalzburg Fortress:

History and Architecture:

Hohensalzburg Fortress was originally built in 1077 by Archbishop Gebhard as a defensive stronghold. Over the centuries, it underwent several expansions and renovations, resulting in its present-day impressive appearance.

Funicular Ride:

To reach the fortress, visitors can take a funicular ride from the Festungsgasse near the Old Town. The funicular journey offers picturesque views of the city as it ascends to the fortress.

Medieval Courtyard:

The fortress's spacious courtyard is an inviting space surrounded by fortified walls and towers. It serves as a central point for visitors to explore various sections of the fortress.

State Rooms:

The Golden Chamber, Golden Hall, and Golden Staircase are opulent state rooms within the fortress. They are adorned with rich decorations, including intricate wooden ceilings and ornate wall paintings.

Salzburg Bull:

The Salzburg Bull is a large organ located in the Golden Hall. It is one of the oldest and largest surviving mechanical pipe organs in the world.

Marionette Museum:

The fortress houses a unique Marionette Museum, showcasing a collection of historical puppets and exhibits related to puppet theater.

Panorama Terrace:

The fortress's panoramic terrace offers breathtaking views of Salzburg, the Salzach River, and the surrounding mountains. It is a popular spot for capturing stunning photographs.

Festungsgasthof:

Hohensalzburg Fortress also features a restaurant, Festungsgasthof, where visitors can enjoy Austrian cuisine while taking in the magnificent views.

Concerts and Events:

The fortress hosts various concerts and events, adding to its allure as a cultural and historical venue.

Festungsmuseum:

Explore the Festungsmuseum to learn about the history of the fortress, Salzburg's archbishops, and medieval life through exhibits and artifacts.

Mozarts Geburtshaus (Mozart's Birthplace)

Mozarts Geburtshaus, also known as Mozart's Birthplace, is one of Salzburg's most significant landmarks and a must-visit destination for music enthusiasts and history lovers. Located on Getreidegasse, one of Salzburg's most famous shopping streets, this historic building is where the prodigious composer Wolfgang Amadeus Mozart was born on January 27, 1756. Today, the house has been transformed into a museum that offers a captivating glimpse into Mozart's early life and musical genius. Here are some highlights and key features of Mozart's Birthplace:

History of the House:

Mozart's Birthplace was originally purchased by Mozart's father, Leopold Mozart, in 1747. The family lived here for over 26 years, and it was within these walls that Mozart's exceptional musical talent began to flourish.

Museum Exhibits:

The museum showcases an extensive collection of Mozart's personal belongings, family portraits, and original musical instruments. Visitors can see his violin, harpsichord, and a clavichord on which he composed music.

Mozart's Childhood:

Explore the rooms where Mozart spent his early years, gaining insight into his upbringing and the supportive environment that nurtured his musical genius.

The Mozart Family:

Learn about the Mozart family and their significant role in shaping Wolfgang Amadeus Mozart's musical career.

Interactive Displays:

The museum features interactive displays and multimedia presentations that provide an engaging and informative experience for visitors of all ages.

Musical Legacy:

Discover the impact of Mozart's music on the world and the enduring legacy he left behind.

Concerts and Events:

The museum occasionally hosts concerts and music performances, allowing visitors to experience Mozart's music in the very place where he was born.

Souvenir Shop:

The museum's gift shop offers a variety of Mozart-themed souvenirs, including music recordings, books, and memorabilia.

Location:

Situated in the heart of Salzburg's Old Town, Mozart's Birthplace is easily accessible and located near other popular attractions.

Educational Programs:

The museum offers educational programs and workshops for schools and groups, making it a valuable educational resource for visitors of all ages.

Mirabell Palace and Gardens

Mirabell Palace and Gardens are a splendid ensemble of Baroque architecture and landscaped gardens located in the heart of Salzburg, Austria. Built in 1606 by Prince-Archbishop Wolf Dietrich for his mistress, Salome Alt, the palace and its gardens have become one of the city's most iconic landmarks. Here are some highlights and key features of Mirabell Palace and Gardens:

Historic Architecture:

Mirabell Palace boasts exquisite Baroque architecture, featuring ornate facades, stately columns, and decorative elements that exemplify the Baroque style of the time.

Marble Hall:

The Marble Hall inside the palace is renowned for its opulence and serves as a stunning venue for weddings, concerts, and other special events.

Mirabell Gardens:

The beautifully landscaped Mirabell Gardens are laid out in a geometric design with numerous flowerbeds, fountains, sculptures, and hedgerows. The gardens offer breathtaking views of Hohensalzburg Fortress and the surrounding mountains.

Pegasus Fountain:

The central focal point of the gardens is the Pegasus Fountain, an elegant fountain featuring the winged horse Pegasus, surrounded by playful statues of other mythical creatures.

Dwarf Garden (Zwerglgarten):

The Dwarf Garden is a whimsical area within the gardens, filled with playful statues of dwarfs, which were popular among the Baroque aristocracy as symbols of extravagance and whimsy.

Rose Garden:

The Rose Garden, located on the eastern side of the palace, showcases a stunning array of colorful roses during the blooming season.

Sound of Music Connection:

Mirabell Gardens is famous for being one of the filming locations of the iconic movie "The Sound of Music." The scene where the von Trapp children sing "Do-Re-Mi" was filmed in the gardens.

Sculptures and Statues:

Throughout the gardens, you'll find a variety of statues and sculptures, including representations of famous historical figures and mythological characters.

Photo Opportunities:

The gardens offer numerous picturesque spots for photography, making it a favorite spot for both tourists and locals.

Cultural Events:

Mirabell Palace and Gardens are also used as a venue for various cultural events, concerts, and festivals throughout the year.

Salzburg Cathedral (Salzburger Dom)

Salzburg Cathedral, known as Salzburger Dom in German, is a magnificent Baroque cathedral and one of the most important religious and architectural landmarks in the city. Situated in the heart of Salzburg's Old Town, the cathedral's grandeur and artistic beauty are a testament to the city's historical and cultural significance. Here are some highlights and key features of Salzburg Cathedral:

History and Architecture:

Salzburg Cathedral dates back to the 8th century when it was initially established as a simple basilica. Over the centuries, it underwent multiple reconstructions and expansions, transforming into the Baroque masterpiece we see today.

Baroque Facade:

The cathedral's impressive Baroque facade features twin towers, elegant columns, and intricate ornamentation, making it a striking example of Baroque architecture.

Domplatz (Cathedral Square):

The cathedral's location in Domplatz makes it a prominent landmark in Salzburg's Old Town. The square is a bustling hub, with the cathedral at its center.

Interior Decorations:

Step inside the cathedral to admire its opulent interior, adorned with frescoes, stucco work, and gilded altars. The grand organ is a prominent feature and is often used during services and concerts.

Dome and Ceiling Paintings:

The cathedral's dome is adorned with beautiful paintings that depict scenes from the life of Jesus and other biblical events.

Baptismal Font:

A noteworthy feature inside the cathedral is the baptismal font, a unique example of Gothic art, which was used for the baptism of Wolfgang Amadeus Mozart.

Crypt:

Explore the crypt beneath the cathedral, which houses the tombs of several archbishops of Salzburg.

Services and Events:

Salzburg Cathedral is an active place of worship, hosting regular Masses, ceremonies, and special events.

Concerts and Music Performances:

The cathedral's acoustics make it an exceptional venue for concerts and music performances, attracting musicians and audiences from around the world.

Christmas and Easter Celebrations:

The cathedral is at the center of Salzburg's Christmas and Easter celebrations, with special services and events taking place during these festive seasons.

Mozarts Wohnhaus (Mozart's Residence)

Mozarts Wohnhaus, or Mozart's Residence, is another significant landmark in Salzburg associated with the life and music of Wolfgang Amadeus Mozart. Located just a short walk from Mozart's Birthplace on Makartplatz, this historic building served as the residence of the Mozart family from 1773 to 1787. Today, the house has been transformed into a museum that offers a comprehensive look at Mozart's later years and his prolific musical career. Here are some highlights and key features of Mozarts Wohnhaus:

Historical Significance:

Mozarts Wohnhaus is where the Mozart family moved when Wolfgang was 17 years old. It was during his time in this residence that he composed many of his greatest works.

Museum Exhibits:

The museum houses an extensive collection of original Mozart family documents, including letters, music manuscripts, and personal belongings.

Compositions and Instruments:

Explore exhibits dedicated to Mozart's compositions and the musical instruments he used to create his masterpieces.

Mozart's Life in Salzburg:

Learn about Mozart's life in Salzburg, his relationships with family and friends, and his experiences as a court musician for the Archbishop of Salzburg.

Interactive Displays:

The museum features interactive displays and multimedia presentations that provide an immersive and informative experience.

The Mozart Family:

Discover more about Mozart's family and the important role they played in his life and career.

Music Room:

The museum has a reconstructed music room, where visitors can imagine Mozart composing and practicing his music.

Temporary Exhibitions:

In addition to its permanent collection, the museum hosts temporary exhibitions related to Mozart's life and music.

Location:

Mozarts Wohnhaus is conveniently located in the city center, making it easy to include in your exploration of Salzburg's historic sites.

Audio Guides and Tours:

Audio guides are available in multiple languages, providing insightful commentary as you explore the museum. Guided tours are also offered for a deeper understanding of Mozart's life and work.

Hellbrunn Palace and Trick Fountains

Hellbrunn Palace, located just a short distance from Salzburg's city center, is a delightful and unique Baroque palace that offers a memorable experience for visitors of all ages. Built between 1612 and 1615 by Prince-Archbishop Markus Sittikus, the palace is renowned for its architectural charm, extensive gardens, and the famous Trick Fountains. Here are some highlights and key features of Hellbrunn Palace and its Trick Fountains:

Architectural Beauty:

Hellbrunn Palace features exquisite Renaissance and Baroque architecture, with playful elements and decorative details that add to its allure.

Trick Fountains:

One of the main highlights of Hellbrunn Palace is the Trick Fountains. Built to entertain and surprise guests during the Archbishop's summer parties, these fountains are full of hidden water jets, grottoes, and whimsical water features.

Wasserspiele (Water Games):

Visitors can join guided tours to experience the fun of the Trick Fountains. Prepare to get wet and be amazed by the creative and ingenious water features.

Palace Gardens:

The palace is surrounded by beautifully landscaped gardens with sculptures, fountains, and walking paths. The gardens are a peaceful and picturesque setting for leisurely strolls.

Hellbrunn Zoo:

Hellbrunn Palace is also home to a small zoo with native animals, offering an enjoyable experience for families and animal lovers.

Gazebo (Pavilion):

The palace gardens feature a charming gazebo, known as the Sound of Music Gazebo, which was featured in the movie "The Sound of Music."

Outdoor Theater:

In the summer, the palace's gardens host cultural events, concerts, and theater performances, providing a unique setting for artistic experiences.

Hellbrunn Castle Museum:

Explore the history and cultural significance of Hellbrunn Palace through exhibits and artifacts in the castle museum.

Salzburg Zoo:

Adjacent to Hellbrunn Palace is the Salzburg Zoo, which is home to a diverse range of animals from around the world.

Location:

Hellbrunn Palace is easily accessible from Salzburg city center, making it a convenient day trip or half-day excursion.

St. Peter's Abbey and Cemetery

St. Peter's Abbey and Cemetery (Stift St. Peter) is one of the oldest and most significant religious landmarks in Salzburg. Located in the heart of the Old Town, the abbey complex is steeped in history and holds cultural and spiritual importance for the city. Here are some highlights and key features of St. Peter's Abbey and Cemetery:

History and Architecture:

Founded in 696 AD, St. Peter's Abbey is one of the oldest monasteries in the German-speaking world. The complex includes a church, monastery buildings, a cemetery, and a library.

St. Peter's Church:

The abbey's church, St. Peter's Church (Peterskirche), is a stunning example of Romanesque and Baroque architecture. It houses beautiful artworks and features a richly decorated interior.

St. Peter's Cemetery:

St. Peter's Cemetery is one of the oldest cemeteries in Salzburg, dating back to the Early Christian era. The cemetery's tranquil setting and historical tombstones make it a unique and atmospheric place.

Catacombs:

Visitors can access the catacombs beneath the abbey, where early Christian and medieval burials took place. The catacombs offer a glimpse into the ancient history of the site.

Stiftskeller St. Peter:

Located within the abbey grounds is Stiftskeller St. Peter, one of the oldest restaurants in Europe, dating back to 803 AD. It offers a traditional dining experience in historic surroundings.

Library:

St. Peter's Abbey Library holds an impressive collection of rare books, manuscripts, and valuable texts, making it a significant cultural and academic resource.

Mozart Connection:

St. Peter's Cemetery is the final resting place of Nannerl Mozart, Wolfgang Amadeus Mozart's sister.

Courtyard and Fountain:

The abbey's inner courtyard features a lovely fountain and provides a peaceful place for reflection.

Views of Hohensalzburg Fortress:

From the cemetery and the abbey's grounds, visitors can enjoy panoramic views of Hohensalzburg Fortress.

Concerts and Events:

The abbey hosts concerts, cultural events, and religious ceremonies, contributing to its role as a vibrant center of cultural and spiritual life.

Kapitelplatz and Giant Chess Board

Kapitelplatz is a lively square located in the heart of Salzburg's Old Town, known for its open space, scenic views, and cultural attractions. One of the prominent features of Kapitelplatz is the Giant Chess Board, a popular spot that attracts both locals and tourists alike. Here are some highlights and key features of Kapitelplatz and the Giant Chess Board:

Kapitelplatz Square:

Kapitelplatz is a spacious and picturesque square situated between Salzburg Cathedral (Salzburger Dom) and St. Peter's Abbey. The square is a popular meeting place and a hub for various cultural events and performances.

Giant Chess Board:

The Giant Chess Board is a unique and eye-catching feature of Kapitelplatz. It is an oversized chessboard built directly on the ground, where visitors can play chess using life-sized chess pieces.

Public Chess Matches:

The Giant Chess Board is not only a decorative installation but also a functional one. Locals and tourists often gather here to engage in friendly chess matches, adding a touch of leisure and playfulness to the square.

Spectacular Views:

Kapitelplatz offers stunning views of Salzburg Cathedral, Hohensalzburg Fortress, and the surrounding historic buildings, making it a popular spot for photography and sightseeing.

Cultural Events:

Throughout the year, Kapitelplatz hosts various cultural events, concerts, and performances, contributing to its vibrant atmosphere.

Sound of Music Connection:

Kapitelplatz is also known for its connection to "The Sound of Music" movie. It is the location where the von Trapp family performed "Do-Re-Mi" while dancing around the Pegasus Fountain.

Art Installations:

At times, Kapitelplatz features art installations and temporary exhibits, adding an artistic touch to the square.

Cafés and Restaurants:

The square is surrounded by cafés and restaurants where visitors can relax, enjoy the views, and savor Austrian cuisine.

Proximity to Salzburg's Attractions:

Kapitelplatz is conveniently located within walking distance of other major attractions, making it an ideal starting point for exploring the city's historic sites.

Christmas Market:

During the Advent season, Kapitelplatz hosts a Christmas market, adding to its festive ambiance and providing a charming setting for holiday shopping and celebrations.

Salzburg Tree Tunnel

The Salzburg Tree Tunnel, also known as the Gasslhöhe Green Tunnel or Tree Tunnel Gasslhöhe, is a popular scenic spot in Salzburg, Austria.

The tree tunnel is located along the Gaisberg Mountain road (Gaisberg Landesstraße), which is a mountain pass near Salzburg. As you drive along this road, you'll be surrounded by a picturesque avenue of trees that arch over the road, creating a natural tunnel effect.

The tunnel is formed by rows of tall and beautiful trees, typically adorned with lush green leaves in the summer and colorful foliage during the autumn. The scenery is stunning and has made it a favorite spot for both locals and visitors to take leisurely drives, go for walks, or capture breathtaking photos.

The Gasslhöhe Green Tunnel offers spectacular views of the surrounding mountains and Salzburg city below. It is especially popular during the autumn season when the foliage turns into vibrant shades of red, orange, and yellow, creating a magical and enchanting atmosphere.

If you're visiting Salzburg and have access to a vehicle, taking a drive through the Salzburg Tree Tunnel is highly recommended to experience the natural beauty and tranquility of the area. However, as with any outdoor attraction, it's always best to check current conditions and access information before planning your visit.

HIDDEN GEMS

Salzburg is a city filled with hidden gems, tucked away in its charming streets and corners. These lesser-known treasures offer unique experiences and a chance to explore the city beyond its well-known landmarks. Here are some hidden gems in Salzburg worth discovering:

Petersfriedhof Cemetery

Petersfriedhof Cemetery, also known as St. Peter's Cemetery, is one of the oldest cemeteries in Salzburg, Austria. Located adjacent to St. Peter's Abbey and the Salzburg Cathedral, this historical burial ground holds significant cultural and artistic value. Here are some key highlights of Petersfriedhof Cemetery:

Historical Significance:

Petersfriedhof Cemetery has a rich history that dates back over a thousand years. It is considered one of the oldest Christian cemeteries in the German-speaking world, with some graves dating as far back as the 8th century.

Artistic Tombstones:

The cemetery is renowned for its artistic tombstones, many of which are intricately carved and adorned with symbolic and religious motifs. These beautifully crafted grave markers add to the cemetery's unique and serene atmosphere.

Catacombs:

One of the cemetery's distinctive features is its catacombs, which are carved into the Mönchsberg rock. These catacombs were used as burial sites for the clergy and nobility in past centuries.

Final Resting Place of Notable Figures:

Petersfriedhof Cemetery is the resting place of several notable figures from Salzburg's history, including Mozart's sister Nannerl Mozart, who was buried here in an unmarked grave.

Quiet and Tranquil Setting:

The cemetery's location adjacent to St. Peter's Abbey and the cliffs of Mönchsberg creates a peaceful and serene ambiance, making it an ideal place for contemplation and reflection.

Scenic Views:

The cemetery offers picturesque views of the surrounding Salzburg landscape, including the Salzburg Cathedral and the fortress of Hohensalzburg, adding to its beauty and appeal.

Tourist Attraction:

While Petersfriedhof Cemetery is a cemetery and a place of reverence, it has become a tourist attraction due to its historical significance and artistic tombstones.

Connection to "The Sound of Music":

The cemetery gained additional fame due to its appearance in the movie "The Sound of Music." In one scene, Maria and the von Trapp children hide from the Nazis among the tombstones.

Burial Traditions:

Petersfriedhof Cemetery provides insight into the burial traditions of Salzburg over the centuries and the reverence the city has for its deceased.

Cultural Heritage:

As part of the St. Peter's Abbey complex, Petersfriedhof Cemetery is an essential cultural heritage site in Salzburg, representing the city's spiritual and historical significance.

Nonnberg Abbey

Nonnberg Abbey, or Nonnbergkloster in German, is a historic Benedictine convent located atop the Mönchsberg hill in Salzburg, Austria. Established in the 8th century, it holds the distinction of being one of the oldest women's monasteries in the German-speaking world and is deeply intertwined with Salzburg's cultural and religious history. Here are some key highlights of Nonnberg Abbey:

Historical Significance:

Nonnberg Abbey was founded in 712 by Saint Rupert, the patron saint of Salzburg, making it one of the oldest continuously operating women's monasteries in the German-speaking regions.

Benedictine Order:

The abbey follows the Rule of St. Benedict, an ancient monastic rule that emphasizes prayer, contemplation, and community life.

Location and Views:

Perched on the Mönchsberg hill, Nonnberg Abbey offers stunning views of Salzburg's Old Town and the surrounding landscapes.

Architectural Beauty:

The abbey's architecture showcases a mix of Romanesque, Gothic, and Baroque styles, reflecting the different periods of its construction and renovation.

Courtyard and Gardens:

Nonnberg Abbey features a tranquil courtyard and beautiful gardens, offering a peaceful retreat for the nuns who live there.

Maria von Trapp Connection:

The abbey gained international fame due to its connection with the von Trapp family, whose life story was portrayed in "The Sound of Music." Maria Augusta Kutschera (later known as Maria von Trapp) was a postulant at Nonnberg Abbey before leaving to marry Captain Georg von Trapp.

St. Erentrude Chapel:

Nonnberg Abbey houses the St. Erentrude Chapel, dedicated to the patron saint of Salzburg. The chapel's interior features stunning frescoes and beautiful Baroque decorations.

Daily Life of the Nuns:

The nuns of Nonnberg Abbey live a contemplative and cloistered life, focusing on prayer, work, and study within the walls of the convent.

Gregorian Chant:

The nuns of Nonnberg Abbey are known for their beautiful Gregorian chant, which has been passed down through generations of the community.

Cultural Heritage:

Nonnberg Abbey is a cherished cultural heritage site in Salzburg, reflecting the city's religious traditions and offering a glimpse into the lives of its devoted community of nuns.

Müllner Bräu Brewery & Beer Garden

Müllner Bräu Brewery and Beer Garden, known as "Müllner Bräu" in German, is a historic brewery and beer garden located in Salzburg, Austria. Situated along the Salzach River, it offers a delightful and authentic Austrian beer experience. Here are some key highlights of Müllner Bräu Brewery and Beer Garden:

Historic Brewery:

Müllner Bräu is one of Salzburg's oldest breweries, with a history dating back to the 14th century. It has been producing traditional Austrian beer for centuries, making it a cherished part of Salzburg's brewing heritage.

Authentic Austrian Beer:

The brewery offers a selection of locally brewed beers, including lagers, ales, and seasonal specialties. Visitors can savor the unique flavors of Austrian beer in a historic and authentic setting.

Beer Garden Ambiance:

The beer garden at Müllner Bräu provides a relaxed and inviting atmosphere, making it an ideal spot to enjoy a cold beer on a warm day or evening.

Scenic Location:

Müllner Bräu's location along the Salzach River offers picturesque views of the water and the surrounding cityscape, adding to the overall beer garden experience.

Traditional Austrian Cuisine:

In addition to its beers, Müllner Bräu serves traditional Austrian dishes, allowing visitors to pair their beer with local culinary delights.

Social Gathering Spot:

The beer garden is a popular spot for both locals and tourists to come together, enjoy the company of friends and family, and experience the conviviality of Austrian beer culture.

Live Music and Events:

During the summer months, Müllner Bräu hosts live music performances and special events, creating a lively and festive atmosphere for visitors.

Brewery Tours:

The brewery offers guided tours that provide insight into the beer-making process and the brewery's history, offering a behind-the-scenes look at the craft of brewing.

Family-Friendly:

Müllner Bräu is a family-friendly venue, welcoming guests of all ages to enjoy the beer garden ambiance and the company of others.

Cultural Experience:

Visiting Müllner Bräu Brewery and Beer Garden offers a unique cultural experience, allowing visitors to immerse themselves in the beer-drinking traditions and local beer culture of Salzburg.

Stieglkeller

Stieglkeller is a historic beer garden and restaurant located on the Mönchsberg hill in Salzburg, Austria. It is one of the city's most iconic and popular spots for both locals and tourists, offering a unique and memorable experience. Here are some key highlights of Stieglkeller:

Historic Setting:

Stieglkeller is situated on the Mönchsberg hill, providing visitors with stunning panoramic views of Salzburg's Old Town, the fortress of Hohensalzburg, and the surrounding landscapes.

Stiegl Brewery:

Stieglkeller is closely associated with Stiegl Brewery, one of Austria's oldest and most renowned breweries. It offers a wide selection of Stiegl beers, including a range of traditional and craft brews.

Beer Garden Ambiance:

The beer garden at Stieglkeller is the perfect place to enjoy a cold beer while soaking in the beautiful views and the fresh alpine air. It is a lively and convivial spot, attracting locals and visitors alike.

Traditional Austrian Cuisine:

Stieglkeller serves a delicious array of traditional Austrian dishes, providing guests with an opportunity to savor authentic Salzburg cuisine.

Gmachl Cellar:

The Gmachl Cellar at Stieglkeller is a unique event venue housed in a historic vaulted cellar. It hosts various cultural events, including live music performances and art exhibitions.

Terrace and Outdoor Seating:

The terrace and outdoor seating areas offer a delightful setting to enjoy meals and drinks in the sunshine or under the stars.

Scenic Hiking Trails:

Stieglkeller is accessible by a scenic hiking trail that leads up the Mönchsberg hill, providing visitors with the option to combine their visit with a pleasant hike.

History and Tradition:

The beer garden has a rich history, dating back to the 15th century when it was established as a brewery. Today, it continues to embrace its traditions while offering a contemporary and enjoyable experience.

Local Music and Culture:

Stieglkeller occasionally hosts live music performances, showcasing local talent and cultural entertainment.

Family-Friendly Atmosphere:

Stieglkeller welcomes families, making it a great spot for a relaxed and enjoyable outing for all ages.

Kaffee-Alchemie

Kaffee-Alchemie is a charming and quirky coffee shop located in Salzburg, Austria. Situated in the heart of the city, this café offers a unique and magical coffee experience, combining creativity, art, and an enchanting ambiance. Here are some key highlights of Kaffee-Alchemie:

Creative Coffee Drinks:

Kaffee-Alchemie is known for its creatively crafted coffee drinks, taking coffee to the next level with unique and artistic presentations.

Magical Atmosphere:

The café exudes a whimsical and magical atmosphere, with its enchanting décor, fairy lights, and captivating displays that transport visitors into an alchemist's world.

Quirky Interior:

The interior of Kaffee-Alchemie features vintage furnishings, curious objects, and artistic elements, creating an eclectic and intriguing ambiance.

Artistic Latte Art:

The café's baristas are skilled at creating intricate and artistic latte art, turning each cup of coffee into a work of art.

Quaint Outdoor Seating:

Kaffee-Alchemie offers quaint outdoor seating, allowing guests to enjoy their coffee in the charming streets of Salzburg.

Sweet and Savory Treats:

In addition to creative coffee drinks, the café offers a delightful selection of sweet and savory treats, including pastries, cakes, and light snacks.

Artisanal Approach:

The café takes an artisanal approach to coffee, using high-quality beans and ingredients to create exceptional coffee beverages.

Whimsical Events:

Kaffee-Alchemie occasionally hosts whimsical events, adding to the magical experience for visitors.

Social Media Sensation:

The café's unique and creative coffee presentations have made it a sensation on social media, attracting coffee enthusiasts and curious visitors from around the world.

Hidden Gem:

Kaffee-Alchemie is a hidden gem in Salzburg, tucked away in the city's historic streets and offering an offbeat and delightful coffee experience.

Café Bazar

Café Bazar is a renowned traditional Viennese-style café located in Salzburg, Austria. Situated along the Salzach River and overlooking the iconic Hohensalzburg Fortress, this historic café has been a beloved spot for locals and visitors since its establishment in 1909. Here are some key highlights of Café Bazar:

Viennese Café Tradition:

Café Bazar follows the classic Viennese café tradition, known for its elegant ambiance, delicious coffee, and delectable pastries.

Historic Charm:

The café exudes a nostalgic and old-world charm with its historic interiors, antique furnishings, and ornate decorations, creating a welcoming and inviting atmosphere.

Riverfront Location:

Café Bazar's prime location along the Salzach River offers picturesque views of the water and the Hohensalzburg Fortress, making it an ideal spot to enjoy a leisurely break.

Terrace Dining:

The café's outdoor terrace allows guests to enjoy their coffee and pastries in the open air, soaking in the scenic beauty of the river and the cityscape.

Coffee and Pastries:

Café Bazar is renowned for its excellent coffee, served in the traditional Viennese style. It also offers a delightful selection of pastries, cakes, and desserts, perfect for a sweet treat.

Literary Connections:

Over the years, Café Bazar has been a popular meeting place for writers, artists, and intellectuals, adding to its literary and cultural significance.

Live Music:

Café Bazar occasionally hosts live music performances, creating a vibrant and entertaining ambiance for its guests.

Breakfast and Brunch:

The café offers a sumptuous breakfast and brunch menu, making it an ideal spot to start the day with a delicious meal.

Family-Friendly:

Café Bazar welcomes families, providing a family-friendly environment for children and adults to enjoy.

Cultural Heritage:

As one of Salzburg's historic cafés, Café Bazar is considered a cultural heritage site, reflecting the city's rich café culture and culinary traditions.

Mozartsteg Pedestrian Bridge

The Mozartsteg Pedestrian Bridge, also known simply as Mozartsteg, is a picturesque pedestrian bridge in Salzburg, Austria. Spanning across the Salzach River, the bridge connects the historic Old Town (Altstadt) with the newer part of the city, making it a popular crossing point for both locals and tourists. Here are some key highlights of the Mozartsteg Pedestrian Bridge:

Location:

The Mozartsteg Pedestrian Bridge is strategically located near the heart of Salzburg's Old Town, providing easy access to many of the city's famous landmarks and attractions.

Iconic Views:

The bridge offers iconic views of Salzburg's Old Town, the Hohensalzburg Fortress, and the picturesque riverbanks, making it a favorite spot for photography and sightseeing.

Foot and Bicycle Traffic:

As a pedestrian bridge, Mozartsteg is exclusively dedicated to foot traffic and bicycles, ensuring a safe and enjoyable crossing for pedestrians.

Connection to Music and History:

The bridge's name pays tribute to Wolfgang Amadeus Mozart, one of the world's greatest composers, who was born in Salzburg. The name "Mozartsteg" translates to "Mozart Bridge" in English.

Locks of Love:

Like many other romantic bridges, Mozartsteg has become a spot for couples to place padlocks as a symbol of their love and commitment. These "locks of love" add a touch of romance to the bridge's ambiance.

Scenic Walks and Picnics:

The bridge is part of a scenic route along the Salzach River, providing an ideal location for leisurely walks and picnics.

Evening Illumination:

At night, the bridge is beautifully illuminated, creating a magical atmosphere and enhancing its charm.

Festivals and Events:

Throughout the year, Mozartsteg becomes a focal point for various events and festivals, adding to the liveliness of the area.

Access to Museums and Landmarks:

The bridge's central location makes it convenient for visitors to access many of Salzburg's museums, historic sites, and architectural wonders.

Symbol of Salzburg:

As an integral part of Salzburg's urban landscape, Mozartsteg represents the city's blend of history, culture, and modernity, making it a symbol of Salzburg's enduring appeal.

Gwandhaus

Gwandhaus is a hidden gem and a boutique in Salzburg, Austria, that specializes in traditional Austrian clothing. Located in the heart of the Old Town (Altstadt), Gwandhaus offers a unique shopping experience for those interested in embracing Salzburg's cultural heritage through traditional clothing. Here are some key highlights of Gwandhaus:

Traditional Austrian Clothing:

Gwandhaus is dedicated to showcasing and preserving the rich traditions of Austrian clothing, including dirndls (traditional dresses) and lederhosen (traditional leather trousers).

High-Quality Products:

The boutique prides itself on offering high-quality, authentic garments made from premium materials, designed to stand the test of time.

Unique Designs:

Gwandhaus offers a selection of traditional clothing in a variety of styles and designs, catering to both classic and contemporary tastes.

Expert Staff:

The boutique's knowledgeable staff provides personalized assistance and styling advice to help customers find the perfect outfit.

Accessories and Embellishments:

Gwandhaus offers a range of accessories and embellishments to complement traditional clothing, including aprons, blouses, and embroidered details.

Tailoring Services:

The boutique offers custom tailoring services to ensure that garments fit perfectly and suit individual preferences.

Cultural Souvenirs:

Gwandhaus provides an opportunity for visitors to take home authentic cultural souvenirs that embody the spirit of Salzburg's traditional clothing.

Connection to Local Culture:

By offering traditional Austrian clothing, Gwandhaus contributes to preserving and promoting the local cultural heritage of Salzburg.

Suitable for All Occasions:

Whether for special events, festivals, or simply to embrace Salzburg's cultural traditions, Gwandhaus offers clothing suitable for various occasions.

Centrally Located:

Gwandhaus' location in the heart of Salzburg's Old Town makes it easily accessible to visitors exploring the city's historic landmarks and attractions.

Linzer Gasse

Linzer Gasse is a charming and vibrant street located in the heart of Salzburg's Old Town (Altstadt), Austria. It is one of the city's most picturesque and popular pedestrian streets, known for its historic architecture, boutique shops, and delightful eateries. Here are some key highlights of Linzer Gasse:

Pedestrian Zone:

Linzer Gasse is a pedestrian-only street, making it a pleasant and pedestrian-friendly area for strolling, shopping, and dining.

Historic Architecture:

The street is lined with historic buildings that showcase a mix of architectural styles, including Baroque, Renaissance, and Gothic elements. The well-preserved facades add to the street's ambiance.

Boutique Shops:

Linzer Gasse is home to a variety of boutique shops and specialty stores, offering a diverse selection of local products, souvenirs, fashion, and unique finds.

Cafés and Restaurants:

The street is dotted with cozy cafés, charming restaurants, and traditional Austrian eateries. It's a perfect place to enjoy coffee, cakes, or a delightful meal in a picturesque setting.

Local Artisans:

Visitors can find several local artisans and craftsmen showcasing their creations along Linzer Gasse, making it an ideal spot to find unique handmade items.

Music and Street Performers:

Linzer Gasse often hosts street musicians and performers, adding to the lively and vibrant atmosphere.

Historic Fountains:

The street features several historic fountains, such as the Furtwänglerbrunnen, providing an interesting backdrop for photos and relaxation.

Cultural and Culinary Delights:

Linzer Gasse represents a fusion of Salzburg's cultural heritage and culinary delights, offering a true taste of the city's local charm.

Access to Historic Sites:

The street leads to many of Salzburg's iconic landmarks, including the Salzburg Cathedral, Mozart's Birthplace, and the Mirabell Palace, making it a convenient starting point for sightseeing.

Nightlife and Entertainment:

In the evening, Linzer Gasse comes alive with a vibrant nightlife, with various bars, pubs, and entertainment venues welcoming visitors for a fun-filled night out.

Dreifaltigkeitskirche (Holy Trinity Church)

Dreifaltigkeitskirche, also known as the Holy Trinity Church, is a beautiful and historic religious landmark located in the heart of Salzburg, Austria. The church is renowned for its stunning Baroque architecture and its significance in the city's religious and cultural heritage. Here are some key highlights of Dreifaltigkeitskirche:

Baroque Architecture:

Dreifaltigkeitskirche is a prime example of Baroque architecture, featuring a grand façade adorned with elaborate sculptures and intricate details.

Monumental Dome:

The church boasts an impressive dome, which adds to its majestic appearance and draws the attention of visitors and passersby.

Interior Splendor:

Inside the church, visitors are treated to an opulent and richly decorated interior, with ornate altars, beautiful frescoes, and elegant stucco work.

Holy Trinity Theme:

As the name suggests, the church is dedicated to the Holy Trinity, with various symbols and motifs throughout the interior reflecting this theme.

Historical Significance:

Dreifaltigkeitskirche has a long and storied history, dating back to the early 18th century when it was commissioned by Prince-Archbishop Johann Ernst von Thun.

Cultural Heritage:

The church holds significant cultural and religious importance for the people of Salzburg, as it has been a place of worship and spiritual reflection for centuries.

Religious Services and Events:

Dreifaltigkeitskirche continues to serve as an active place of worship, hosting religious services and events for both locals and visitors.

Musical Performances:

The church occasionally hosts musical performances and concerts, taking advantage of its excellent acoustics and majestic setting.

Central Location:

Dreifaltigkeitskirche is conveniently located near other popular attractions in Salzburg, making it easily accessible to tourists exploring the city.

Quiet Oasis:

Despite its central location, the church offers a serene and tranquil atmosphere, providing a peaceful escape from the bustling city streets.

MUSEUMS

Salzburg is a city rich in history, culture, and the arts, and its museums reflect this wealth of heritage. From art and music to history and science, the city offers a diverse array of museums that cater to various interests and passions. Here are some of the notable museums in Salzburg:

Museum der Moderne Salzburg (Museum of Modern Art)

The Museum der Moderne Salzburg, also known as the Museum of Modern Art, is a prominent cultural institution in Salzburg, Austria. Situated on the Mönchsberg, a hill overlooking the city, the museum showcases an impressive collection of modern and contemporary art. With its stunning hilltop location and diverse exhibitions, the Museum der Moderne is a popular destination for art enthusiasts and visitors seeking an immersive cultural experience. Here are some key highlights of the Museum der Moderne Salzburg:

Hilltop Location:

The museum is situated on the Mönchsberg, providing visitors with breathtaking views of Salzburg's Old Town and the surrounding landscapes. Its unique hilltop position adds to the allure of the museum.

Modern and Contemporary Art:

The Museum der Moderne is dedicated to modern and contemporary art, featuring works from the late 19th century to the present day. The collection includes paintings, sculptures, photographs, installations, and video art by Austrian and international artists.

Changing Exhibitions:

The museum hosts rotating exhibitions that cover a wide range of artistic styles and themes. From modernist masterpieces to cutting-edge contemporary art, visitors can explore a diverse array of artworks during their visit.

Sammlung Friedrichshof Collection:

The museum houses the Sammlung Friedrichshof Collection, a significant ensemble of contemporary art amassed by the Friedrichshof Foundation. This collection includes works by artists such as Gustav Klimt, Egon Schiele, and Oskar Kokoschka.

Mönchsberg Terrace:

The museum's Mönchsberg Terrace offers a perfect spot to take in panoramic views of Salzburg, the Hohensalzburg Fortress, and the Salzach River.

Architecture and Design:

The Museum der Moderne Salzburg is an architectural gem itself, designed by Friedrich Hoff Zwink and opened in 2004. Its modern architecture complements the natural beauty of the Mönchsberg and provides an inviting space for art appreciation.

Guided Tours and Workshops:

The museum offers guided tours and educational workshops that enhance the visitor experience and provide deeper insights into the art on display.

Events and Cultural Programs:

The museum organizes various events, lectures, and cultural programs, enriching the art experience and fostering a dynamic artistic community.

Salzburg Museum

The Salzburg Museum is a prominent cultural institution dedicated to preserving and showcasing the history, art, and cultural heritage of Salzburg and its surrounding region. Situated in the heart of the city, the museum provides visitors with a comprehensive and engaging exploration of Salzburg's past and present. Here are some key highlights of the Salzburg Museum:

Historical Significance:

The Salzburg Museum has a long history, dating back to its founding in 1834. Over the years, it has grown and evolved, expanding its collection and exhibitions to reflect the city's rich cultural heritage.

State-of-the-Art Exhibitions:

The museum features state-of-the-art exhibitions that cover various aspects of Salzburg's history, culture, and art. Its curated displays provide visitors with a detailed and immersive experience of the city's past and present.

Archaeological Finds:

The museum houses an extensive collection of archaeological artifacts that offer insights into the region's prehistoric and Roman past. Visitors can see ancient relics, sculptures, and everyday objects that provide a glimpse into Salzburg's ancient history.

Historical Artworks:

The museum boasts an impressive collection of historical artworks, including paintings, sculptures, and decorative arts from different periods in Salzburg's history.

Salzburg in the 20th Century:

The museum dedicates a section to Salzburg's history in the 20th century, highlighting significant events and developments that shaped the city during this transformative period.

Multimedia Installations:

In addition to traditional exhibits, the Salzburg Museum features multimedia installations and interactive displays that engage visitors and enhance their understanding of the content.

Temporary Exhibitions:

The museum regularly hosts temporary exhibitions that focus on various themes, from contemporary art to cultural topics, offering fresh and dynamic perspectives.

Mozart and Salzburg's Musical Heritage:

As the birthplace of Wolfgang Amadeus Mozart, Salzburg's musical heritage is an integral part of the city's identity. The museum features exhibits related to Mozart's life and works, celebrating his enduring legacy.

Interactive Programs and Events:

The Salzburg Museum offers interactive programs and events for all ages, including workshops, lectures, and guided tours that provide a deeper appreciation of Salzburg's cultural heritage.

Panorama Museum:

Located within the Salzburg Museum, the Panorama Museum showcases a circular painting that offers a panoramic view of Salzburg in the 19th century.

Mozart's Birthplace (Mozarts Geburtshaus)

Mozart's Birthplace, known as "Mozarts Geburtshaus" in German, is one of the most significant landmarks in Salzburg and a popular destination for music lovers and history enthusiasts from around the world. Located in the heart of the city on Getreidegasse, the house where Wolfgang Amadeus Mozart was born on January 27, 1756, has been preserved as a museum dedicated to the life and works of the famous composer. Here are some key highlights of Mozart's Birthplace:

Historical Significance:

Mozart's Birthplace holds immense historical and cultural significance as the place where one of the greatest composers in history was born and spent his early years. It provides a tangible connection to Mozart's life and the city that shaped his musical genius.

Museum Exhibits:

The museum's exhibits offer a fascinating insight into Mozart's early life, family, and musical journey. Visitors can explore the rooms where Mozart and his family lived, see authentic documents, and view original instruments that belonged to the composer.

Family Memorabilia:

The museum houses a collection of family memorabilia, including personal belongings, letters, and portraits of Mozart and his family members, providing a glimpse into their daily lives.

Musical Legacy:

The museum highlights Mozart's musical achievements, featuring manuscripts, compositions, and audio displays of his famous works, showcasing the breadth of his talent and artistic contribution.

Guided Tours:

Guided tours are available to provide visitors with a deeper understanding of Mozart's life, his connection to Salzburg, and the historical context of his era.

Commemorative Events:

The museum hosts various events and concerts to celebrate Mozart's legacy, attracting music enthusiasts and musicians from around the world.

Location:

Mozart's Birthplace is conveniently situated in the heart of Salzburg's Old Town, making it easily accessible for tourists exploring the city's historic landmarks.

Musical Instruments:

The museum houses a collection of Mozart's original instruments, including his childhood violin, providing a direct link to the composer's musical beginnings.

The Mozart Family:

The museum sheds light on the talented and influential Mozart family, which played a significant role in shaping Wolfgang's musical upbringing and career.

Legacy of Inspiration:

As one of Salzburg's most visited attractions, Mozart's Birthplace continues to inspire visitors with its celebration of artistic brilliance and the enduring legacy of Wolfgang Amadeus Mozart.

Mozart's Residence (Mozarts Wohnhaus)

Mozart's Residence, known as "Mozarts Wohnhaus" in German, is another important museum in Salzburg dedicated to the life and legacy of Wolfgang Amadeus Mozart. The museum is situated just a few minutes' walk from Mozart's Birthplace on Makartplatz and is housed in the building where the Mozart family lived from 1773 to 1787. This period was significant in Mozart's career, as he composed many of his renowned works during his time at this residence. Here are some key highlights of Mozart's Residence:

Historical Significance:

Mozart's Residence holds great historical significance as the place where Mozart lived and worked during some of the most productive years of his life. It provides visitors with an intimate connection to the composer's daily life and creative endeavors.

Museum Exhibits:

The museum features exhibits that offer insights into Mozart's life in Salzburg, his family dynamics, and the historical context of the late 18th century. Visitors can explore the various rooms where the Mozart family lived, including Mozart's former music room and his father's workshop.

Mozart's Compositions:

The museum showcases some of Mozart's most significant compositions, manuscripts, and documents, illustrating his creative process and musical genius.

Musical Instruments:

Mozart's Residence houses a collection of musical instruments, including pianos and violins, which provide visitors with a sense of the composer's musical environment.

Guided Tours:

Guided tours are available to offer visitors a deeper understanding of Mozart's life, his family's role in his career, and the social and musical context of his time.

Makartplatz Square:

The museum's location on Makartplatz Square offers a picturesque setting and a vibrant atmosphere in the heart of Salzburg.

Temporary Exhibitions:

Mozart's Residence hosts temporary exhibitions that focus on different aspects of Mozart's life, his travels, and his musical legacy.

Musical Events:

The museum occasionally hosts concerts and musical events that celebrate Mozart's works and the rich musical heritage of Salzburg.

Souvenir Shop:

A souvenir shop within the museum offers visitors the opportunity to take home mementos and music-related memorabilia.

Cultural Heritage:

Mozart's Residence serves as an essential cultural heritage site in Salzburg, preserving and promoting the legacy of one of the most influential composers in the history of classical music.

Salzburg Cathedral Museum (Dommuseum Salzburg)

The Salzburg Cathedral Museum, also known as "Dommuseum Salzburg" in German, is a significant cultural institution located in the heart of Salzburg. Housed in the former residence of the prince-archbishops, the museum is adjacent to Salzburg Cathedral (Salzburger Dom) and offers a captivating journey through the city's ecclesiastical and artistic history. Here are some key highlights of the Salzburg Cathedral Museum:

Historical Significance:

The museum is situated in the Residenzplatz, next to Salzburg Cathedral, and is housed in the Residenz Palace, which served as the official residence of the prince-archbishops of Salzburg.

Art and Artifacts:

The Salzburg Cathedral Museum features a vast collection of religious art and artifacts, including sculptures, paintings, vestments, and liturgical objects. The exhibits span various periods, from the Middle Ages to the Baroque era.

Salzburg Cathedral Treasury:

The museum houses the Salzburg Cathedral Treasury, which displays an impressive assortment of religious treasures, including precious metalwork, reliquaries, and sacred vessels.

Ecclesiastical History:

The museum provides insights into the religious and ecclesiastical history of Salzburg, showcasing the role of the prince-archbishops and the importance of the cathedral in the city's spiritual and cultural life.

Religious Art and Sculptures:

Visitors can admire a wide range of religious art and sculptures, with works by renowned artists such as Tilman Riemenschneider and Martin Johann Schmidt (Kremser Schmidt).

Temporary Exhibitions:

In addition to its permanent collection, the museum hosts temporary exhibitions that focus on specific themes and aspects of Salzburg's religious and cultural heritage.

Guided Tours:

Guided tours are available to provide visitors with a deeper understanding of the museum's exhibits, the history of Salzburg Cathedral, and the significance of the religious art on display.

Cultural Heritage:

The Salzburg Cathedral Museum serves as an essential custodian of the city's cultural heritage, preserving and promoting the artistic and religious legacy of Salzburg.

Multimedia Presentations:

The museum incorporates multimedia presentations and interactive displays, enhancing the visitor experience and offering additional context to the exhibits.

Location:

The museum's location in the heart of Salzburg's historic center makes it easily accessible to visitors exploring the city's renowned landmarks and attractions.

Toy Museum (Spielzeugmuseum)

The Toy Museum, known as "Spielzeugmuseum" in German, is a delightful cultural institution in Salzburg that offers a journey into the world of toys, games, and childhood play. Housed in the historical Old Town, the museum showcases an extensive collection of toys and games from different periods, providing visitors with a nostalgic and enchanting experience. Here are some key highlights of the Toy Museum in Salzburg:

Historical Collection:

The museum features a diverse and extensive collection of toys and games from various eras, offering insights into the history of play and childhood pastimes.

Toys from Different Cultures:

In addition to Austrian toys, the museum exhibits toys and games from different cultures, providing a broader perspective on the universal nature of play.

Interactive Exhibits:

The museum offers interactive exhibits that allow visitors, both young and old, to engage with the toys and games on display, making the experience immersive and entertaining.

Antique Dolls and Teddy Bears:

Antique dolls and teddy bears are among the highlights of the museum's collection, evoking feelings of nostalgia and sentimental value.

Miniature Worlds:

The Toy Museum features miniature worlds and dollhouses that showcase meticulous craftsmanship and attention to detail.

Educational Value:

The museum offers educational value, providing historical context and cultural insights into the toys and games of the past.

Toy Workshops and Activities:

The museum occasionally hosts toy workshops and interactive activities for children, encouraging creativity and imaginative play.

Child-Friendly Atmosphere:

The Toy Museum creates a child-friendly atmosphere, making it an enjoyable and family-friendly destination in Salzburg.

Gift Shop:

The museum's gift shop offers a selection of toy-related souvenirs and memorabilia, providing visitors with the opportunity to take home a piece of childhood joy.

Central Location:

The Toy Museum's location in the heart of Salzburg's Old Town makes it easily accessible to visitors exploring other attractions in the historic center.

Panorama Museum Salzburg

The Panorama Museum Salzburg, known as "Panorama Museum Salzburg" in German, is a unique cultural institution that offers visitors a captivating visual experience. Situated within the city of Salzburg, the museum is dedicated to showcasing the Panorama of the City of Salzburg, a large panoramic painting that provides a 360-degree view of the city in the year 1829. Here are some key highlights of the Panorama Museum Salzburg:

Panorama Painting:

The centerpiece of the museum is the Panorama of the City of Salzburg, a monumental circular painting that depicts the city as it appeared in the early 19th century. Painted by Johann Michael Sattler, the panorama measures 26 meters in length and 3.6 meters in height, creating a captivating and immersive visual experience for visitors.

Historical Accuracy:

The panorama is renowned for its historical accuracy and attention to detail. It offers a fascinating glimpse into the city's architecture, streets, landmarks, and daily life during the early 19th century.

360-Degree Perspective:

The circular format of the painting provides visitors with a unique 360-degree perspective of Salzburg, allowing them to step into the scene and feel as though they are part of the historical moment.

Interactive Display:

The museum incorporates modern technology to enhance the visitor experience. Interactive displays and audio guides offer additional context and information about the panorama and the city's history.

Historical Context:

The museum provides historical context to the panorama, explaining the artistic techniques used by Johann Michael Sattler to create this extraordinary work of art.

Audiovisual Presentation:

The museum offers audiovisual presentations that provide insights into the creation of the panorama and its significance as a historical representation of the city.

Location:

The Panorama Museum Salzburg is conveniently located in the heart of the city, making it easily accessible to visitors exploring other attractions in Salzburg's historic center.

Educational Value:

The panorama painting offers educational value for both locals and tourists, providing a vivid glimpse into Salzburg's past and serving as a valuable historical record.

Cultural Experience:

A visit to the Panorama Museum Salzburg offers a cultural experience that combines art, history, and technology, allowing visitors to step back in time and immerse themselves in the city's rich heritage.

City Views:

The museum's location on the Mönchsberg allows visitors to enjoy panoramic views of Salzburg's Old Town and the surrounding landscapes, adding to the overall experience.

Salzburg Baroque Museum

The Salzburg Baroque Museum, known as "Salzburg Barockmuseum" in German, is a cultural institution dedicated to showcasing the artistic and cultural heritage of the Baroque period in Salzburg. Housed in the Neue Residenz building, which itself is a splendid example of Baroque architecture, the museum offers visitors an immersive experience into the opulence and creativity of the Baroque era. Here are some key highlights of the Salzburg Baroque Museum:

Baroque Art and Decorative Arts:

The museum features an extensive collection of Baroque art, including paintings, sculptures, and decorative objects that exemplify the grandeur and richness of the Baroque style.

Neue Residenz:

The museum is located in the Neue Residenz, a magnificent Baroque palace that served as the residence of the prince-archbishops of Salzburg. The palace itself is a work of art, with lavish interior decorations and elegant architecture.

Baroque Period in Salzburg:

The museum provides insights into Salzburg's prominence during the Baroque period, which saw a flourishing of artistic and cultural achievements under the rule of the prince-archbishops.

Religious Art:

Baroque art often had strong religious themes, and the museum showcases a selection of religious paintings, altarpieces, and sculptures from the period.

Salzburg's Baroque Artists:

The museum highlights the works of prominent Baroque artists who lived and worked in Salzburg, including painters, sculptors, and architects.

Decorative Arts and Furnishings:

The Salzburg Baroque Museum also features decorative arts and furnishings from the Baroque period, providing a glimpse into the luxurious lifestyle of the time.

Special Exhibitions:

In addition to its permanent collection, the museum hosts special exhibitions that focus on specific aspects of the Baroque era, offering visitors a diverse range of artistic and cultural experiences.

Guided Tours and Educational Programs:

The museum offers guided tours and educational programs for visitors of all ages, providing a deeper understanding of the Baroque art and history.

Cultural Events:

The museum occasionally hosts cultural events, concerts, and lectures that celebrate the Baroque era and its influence on Salzburg's history.

Central Location:

The Salzburg Baroque Museum's central location in the heart of the city makes it easily accessible to visitors exploring other attractions in the historic center.

St. Peter's Abbey Museum (Stift St. Peter)

St. Peter's Abbey Museum, also known as "Stift St. Peter" in German, is a captivating cultural institution located in the heart of Salzburg's Old Town. Situated within the grounds of St. Peter's Abbey, one of the oldest monasteries in the German-speaking world, the museum offers visitors a fascinating journey through the abbey's rich history, art, and cultural heritage. Here are some key highlights of St. Peter's Abbey Museum:

Historical Significance:

St. Peter's Abbey is one of the oldest continuously operating monasteries in the German-speaking world, with a history dating back over 1,200 years. The museum provides insights into the abbey's pivotal role in Salzburg's spiritual and cultural development.

Art and Architecture:

The museum showcases a remarkable collection of religious art, including paintings, sculptures, and liturgical objects, which reflect the abbey's cultural and artistic legacy.

Manuscripts and Rare Books:

St. Peter's Abbey Museum houses a valuable collection of manuscripts and rare books, many of which are of significant historical and religious importance.

Baroque Library:

The abbey's Baroque library is an architectural gem, featuring beautifully adorned bookshelves and an impressive collection of historic books and writings.

Historical Artefacts:

Visitors can view historical artefacts, including medieval religious artifacts and ecclesiastical treasures, providing a glimpse into the abbey's religious practices.

Monastery Courtyard:

The museum is located within the monastery courtyard, surrounded by elegant cloisters and peaceful gardens, creating a serene and contemplative atmosphere.

St. Peter's Cemetery:

Adjacent to the abbey is the St. Peter's Cemetery, one of the oldest cemeteries in Salzburg, with artistic tombstones and the catacombs carved into the Mönchsberg rock.

Guided Tours:

Guided tours are available, providing visitors with a deeper understanding of the abbey's history, the religious significance of the artworks, and the daily life of the monks.

Cultural Events:

St. Peter's Abbey Museum occasionally hosts cultural events, including concerts and exhibitions, adding to the richness of the visitor experience.

Central Location:

The museum's central location in the heart of Salzburg's historic center makes it easily accessible to visitors exploring other attractions in the area.

SCULPTURES, STATUES AND MONUMENTS

Salzburg, Austria, is home to several beautiful sculptures, statues, and monuments that add to the city's cultural and artistic heritage. Here are some notable ones to explore:

Residenz Fountain (Residenzbrunnen)

The Residenz Fountain (Residenzbrunnen) is a magnificent Baroque fountain located in Residenzplatz, a large square in the heart of Salzburg, Austria. The fountain is one of the most significant and visually striking landmarks in the city.

The Residenz Fountain was constructed in 1661 by Tommaso di Garone, an Italian architect and sculptor. It was commissioned by Prince Archbishop Guidobald von Thun as part of his efforts to beautify the city and demonstrate its wealth and cultural sophistication.

The fountain features a central group of statues depicting the goddess Diana, the Roman goddess of the hunt, surrounded by other mythological figures, including Neptune, the god of the sea, Tritons, and nymphs. The figures are elegantly sculpted and intricately detailed, reflecting the exceptional craftsmanship of the Baroque period.

The fountain's water flows from a shell held by the central figure of Diana, cascading down into a large basin below. The basin is adorned with various decorative elements, including cherubs and dolphins.

In the past, the Residenz Fountain served as an essential water source for residents and visitors in Salzburg. Today, it remains a popular attraction and a symbol of the city's Baroque architectural heritage.

The Residenz Fountain is surrounded by several historic buildings, including the Salzburg Residence (Residenz), the former palace of the Prince Archbishops, and the Salzburg Cathedral (Salzburger Dom). Together, these landmarks create a grand and impressive architectural ensemble in Residenzplatz, making it one of the most beautiful squares in Salzburg.

Visitors to Salzburg can enjoy the Residenz Fountain and its stunning Baroque sculptures while exploring the city's historic center and learning about its rich cultural history.

Pegasus Fountain (Pegasusbrunnen)

The Pegasus Fountain (Pegasusbrunnen) is another beautiful fountain located in Salzburg, Austria. It can be found in the picturesque Mirabell Gardens (Mirabellgarten), which is a part of the Mirabell Palace complex.

The Pegasus Fountain was designed in the late 17th century by the Italian sculptor Ottavio Mosto. It was commissioned by Prince Archbishop Johann Ernst von Thun and was completed in 1913. The fountain features a statue of Pegasus, the mythical winged horse from Greek mythology, which is the centerpiece of the fountain.

In the sculpture, Pegasus is shown standing on his hind legs, with his wings spread wide. Water cascades from Pegasus's mouth and flows down into the fountain's basin. The fountain is adorned with other decorative elements, including cherubs and dolphins, adding to its beauty and artistic charm.

The Mirabell Gardens, where the Pegasus Fountain is situated, are renowned for their exquisite design and landscaping. The gardens were originally laid out in the early 18th century and were part of the Mirabell Palace complex, which was a symbol of love and devotion by Prince Archbishop Johann Ernst von Thun to his mistress, Salome Alt.

Today, the Mirabell Gardens are a popular destination for both locals and tourists, offering a peaceful and enchanting environment for leisurely strolls and relaxation. The Pegasus Fountain is one of the main attractions within the gardens, and visitors often enjoy capturing its elegance and grace through photographs.

The combination of the Pegasus Fountain, the beautifully landscaped gardens, and the impressive Mirabell Palace in the background makes the Mirabell Gardens an ideal spot for visitors to experience the historic and artistic charm of Salzburg.

Sebastian Staircase Sculptures

The Sebastian Staircase Sculptures, also known as the St. Sebastian Cemetery Sculptures, are a set of striking sculptures located on the stairs leading up to the Hohensalzburg Fortress in Salzburg, Austria. The sculptures are positioned along the staircase known as the "Steingasse" staircase or "Sebastiansstiege."

The staircase is named after St. Sebastian, who is often depicted in Christian art as a martyr pierced by arrows. The sculptures are a series of statues representing scenes from the life of Saint Sebastian, as well as other religious figures and symbols.

The exact origins of these sculptures are not entirely clear, but they are believed to have been created in the late 17th or early 18th century. The artist behind the sculptures remains unknown, adding an air of mystery to this artistic ensemble.

The figures along the Sebastian Staircase are carved from stone and are skillfully crafted, capturing intricate details and expressions. The statues' positioning along the staircase creates a dramatic and visually impactful experience for those ascending to the Hohensalzburg Fortress.

The staircase is not only an architectural and artistic treasure but also offers panoramic views of Salzburg and the surrounding landscape. Many visitors to Salzburg take the time to climb the Sebastian Staircase to appreciate both the sculptures and the breathtaking scenery.

The combination of the historic significance, the artistic beauty of the sculptures, and the stunning views makes the Sebastian Staircase an essential stop for those exploring Salzburg's cultural and historical heritage.

Kapitelschwemme

The Kapitelschwemme is a beautiful Baroque fountain located in Kapitelplatz, a square in the heart of Salzburg, Austria. It is one of the city's notable landmarks and a fine example of Baroque architectural and artistic style.

The Kapitelschwemme was constructed in the early 18th century during the reign of Prince Archbishop Johann Ernst von Thun. It was designed by the Italian sculptor and architect Tommaso di Garone, who also worked on other architectural projects in Salzburg.

The fountain's name, "Kapitelschwemme," translates to "Chapter Fountain" in English, referring to its proximity to Salzburg Cathedral (Salzburger Dom) and its connection to the cathedral's chapter (group of clergy members).

The design of the Kapitelschwemme fountain is ornate and elaborate, typical of the Baroque period. It features a central figure of the Virgin Mary standing on a pedestal, holding the Christ Child. The statue of Mary is surrounded by a semi-circular wall with a series of niches, each containing a statue of a saint or a religious figure.

The water in the Kapitelschwemme flows from spouts held by the saints, and the fountain served as a water source for the people of Salzburg during the past. The architectural details, intricate carvings, and religious significance make it a captivating work of art.

The Kapitelschwemme is a popular spot for both locals and tourists to take a moment to appreciate its beauty and historical significance. The fountain stands as a testament to

Salzburg's Baroque heritage and the city's rich artistic and cultural past.

Mozart Monument

The Mozart Monument is a famous statue located in the city of Salzburg, Austria, dedicated to the renowned composer Wolfgang Amadeus Mozart. The statue is one of the most iconic landmarks in Salzburg and is situated in Mozartplatz, a square in the heart of the city's historic center.

The Mozart Monument was unveiled in 1842 to commemorate the 50th anniversary of Mozart's death. It was sculpted by Ludwig Schwanthaler, a German sculptor, and it depicts Mozart in a graceful and noble pose. The bronze statue shows Mozart holding a quill in his right hand, symbolizing his musical genius as a composer, and a music sheet in his left hand, representing his lifelong passion for music.

The monument has become a significant symbol of Salzburg's cultural heritage and its association with Wolfgang Amadeus Mozart, who was born in the city in 1756. The statue stands in front of the Salzburg Residence, an impressive historic building that was once the residence of the ruling Prince-Archbishops of Salzburg.

Mozartplatz, where the monument is located, is a popular gathering place for locals and tourists alike, and it serves as a venue for various cultural events and performances, especially during the annual Salzburg Festival.

The Mozart Monument continues to be a cherished site for music enthusiasts and history lovers, paying tribute to one of the most celebrated and influential composers in classical music history. It serves as a reminder of Mozart's enduring legacy and the impact of his musical genius on the world of music.

Monument to Hans Makart

The Monument to Hans Makart is a sculpture located in Salzburg, Austria, dedicated to the renowned Austrian painter Hans Makart. It is situated in Makartplatz, a square named after the artist.

Hans Makart was a prominent painter of the 19th century and was associated with the historicism and academic art movements. He was born in Salzburg in 1840 and achieved great success and recognition during his lifetime. Makart's work was known for its grandiosity, vivid colors, and attention to detail.

The monument was unveiled in 1889, four years after Makart's death, to honor his artistic contributions and celebrate his legacy in his hometown. The sculpture was created by the Austrian sculptor Caspar von Zumbusch.

The monument portrays Makart in a seated position on a pedestal, dressed in a robe, and holding a palette and brush, symbolizing his role as an artist. The sculptural depiction captures the essence of his artistic spirit and achievements.

Makartplatz, where the monument stands, is a central square in Salzburg, located not far from Mirabell Gardens and the Mirabell Palace. The square and the monument serve as a tribute to the significant impact Makart had on the art world and as a reminder of Salzburg's artistic heritage.

Today, the Monument to Hans Makart remains a notable landmark and an important symbol of Salzburg's cultural and artistic history, attracting visitors interested in the city's artistic heritage and the life and works of the influential Austrian painter.

University Square Statue (Universitätsplatz)

This square, known as Universitätsplatz (University Square), is home to a notable statue of the famous theologian, philosopher, and scientist, Paracelsus. Paracelsus, whose real name was Philippus Aureolus Theophrastus Bombastus von Hohenheim, was a highly influential figure during the Renaissance period and is considered one of the founding fathers of modern medicine and pharmacology.

The statue of Paracelsus stands as a tribute to his remarkable contributions to various fields of knowledge. It depicts him in a dignified pose, holding a book and with a thoughtful expression on his face, symbolizing his commitment to learning and understanding the secrets of nature.

Paracelsus was a controversial figure in his time, as he challenged the traditional medical practices and beliefs of the medieval era. He advocated for the use of observations and experimentation in medicine, which was a revolutionary concept at the time. His approach emphasized the importance of the human body's interaction with its environment and the use of natural substances in medical treatments.

Beyond medicine, Paracelsus also made significant contributions to alchemy, astrology, and theology. He sought to bridge the gap between science and spirituality, believing that both were interconnected and vital for the advancement of knowledge.

The statue of Paracelsus in Universitätsplatz serves as a reminder of the great thinkers and innovators who have shaped Salzburg's intellectual and cultural landscape. It is a symbol of the city's commitment to education, research, and the pursuit of knowledge.

As visitors and locals gather in Universitätsplatz, they are met with the inspiring presence of Paracelsus, a towering figure of intellect and curiosity. The statue stands as a testament to the enduring legacy of this Renaissance polymath, inviting all who pass by to reflect on the importance of science, philosophy, and spirituality in shaping our understanding of the world. Universitätsplatz and its statue of Paracelsus become a focal point of appreciation for Salzburg's intellectual heritage and its embrace of innovation and inquiry.

Glockenspiel

The term "Glockenspiel" typically refers to a musical instrument or a specific feature in a clock tower that plays a tune using a set of tuned bells or chimes. In the context of Salzburg, Austria, the Glockenspiel is associated with the New Residence (Neue Residenz) building located in Residenzplatz, a square in the heart of the city.

The Glockenspiel in Salzburg is part of the Glockenspiel Tower, which is a notable architectural element of the New Residence. It consists of 35 bells that play a melody at certain times of the day. The Glockenspiel plays various musical pieces, and the figurines on the clock tower also move in time to the music.

One of the most famous melodies played by the Glockenspiel is the "Morgentau" (Morning Dew) song, composed by Leopold Mozart, father of Wolfgang Amadeus Mozart. This musical piece is one of the traditional tunes that delight visitors and residents alike.

The Glockenspiel in Salzburg is a beloved attraction and a popular gathering spot for tourists and locals. Visitors often gather in Residenzplatz to watch and listen to the musical performance of the Glockenspiel, enjoying the delightful tunes and the charming movements of the figurines.

The Glockenspiel is not only an entertaining feature but also a cultural symbol of Salzburg's musical heritage and its connection to the Mozart family. It adds to the city's enchanting atmosphere and serves as a reminder of Salzburg's rich artistic and historical legacy.

Cloak of Conscience

Cloak of Conscience is indeed a sculpture by the Czech sculptor Anna Chromý, and it is located in Salzburg, Austria.

Cloak of Conscience is a captivating and thought-provoking sculpture that depicts a figure shrouded in a flowing cloak. The cloak itself appears as a cascading waterfall, with numerous holes and openings that reveal human figures inside. The figures represent souls seeking enlightenment and self-discovery, symbolizing the ongoing quest for inner truth and conscience.

The sculpture is situated in Kapitelplatz, one of Salzburg's public squares, and it has become an iconic and much-photographed piece of public art in the city. Its profound message and distinctive design have made it a popular attraction for locals and tourists alike.

The Cloak of Conscience sculpture by Anna Chromý is a fascinating addition to Salzburg's artistic and cultural landscape, and it invites viewers to contemplate the deeper meaning of conscience and the complexities of human existence.

Marian Column in Salzburg

The Marian Column in Salzburg, Austria, is a historical monument and a significant example of a Marian Column dedicated to the Virgin Mary. It is located in the Residenzplatz (Residence Square) in the heart of Salzburg.

The Marian Column was erected in 1671 as a symbol of gratitude and religious devotion to the Virgin Mary for her intercession during a plague epidemic that struck the city in the 1670s. The people of Salzburg believed that their prayers to the Virgin Mary helped spare the city from further devastation.

The column features a statue of the Virgin Mary on top, and below her are angels and cherubs. The Marian Column is a beautiful Baroque-style monument with intricate details and artistic embellishments, reflecting the artistic sensibilities of the period.

Wolfgang Hagenauer and Johann Baptist Hagenauer are prominent names associated with the creation of the Marian Column. They were skilled sculptors and artists from the well-known Hagenauer family of craftsmen. Wolfgang Hagenauer was responsible for sculpting the statue of the Virgin Mary atop the column, while Johann Baptist Hagenauer contributed to other artistic elements of the monument.

The Marian Column has become an essential symbol of religious devotion and a historical landmark in Salzburg. It stands as a reminder of the city's past and the significance of faith and art in shaping its cultural heritage.

As with many historical monuments, the Marian Column has likely undergone restoration and conservation efforts over the years to preserve its beauty and historical significance for future generations. It continues to be an important site for both locals and tourists, offering a glimpse into Salzburg's rich history and artistic legacy.

MUSIC AND CULTURE

Music and culture play a central role in Salzburg's identity and allure. As the birthplace of the famous composer Wolfgang Amadeus Mozart, the city has a rich musical heritage that continues to thrive today. Here are some key aspects of music and culture in Salzburg:

Mozart's Legacy

Mozart's legacy is an enduring and profound influence on the world of music and culture. As one of the greatest composers in history, Wolfgang Amadeus Mozart left behind a remarkable body of work that continues to captivate audiences and inspire musicians and artists to this day. His legacy is felt not only in his hometown of Salzburg but throughout the world, shaping the course of classical music and transcending cultural and generational boundaries. Here are some key aspects of Mozart's legacy:

Musical Genius:

Mozart's extraordinary musical talent manifested at an early age, composing his first piece at the age of five and creating masterful compositions throughout his short life. His unparalleled ability to effortlessly craft intricate melodies, harmonies, and structures revolutionized the world of music.

Prolific Output:

Mozart's prodigious output includes over 600 compositions, spanning various genres such as symphonies, operas, chamber music, piano concertos, and more. His diverse body of work showcases his mastery of both instrumental and vocal music.

Influence on Classical Music:

Mozart's innovative compositions and musical language significantly contributed to the development of the Classical period in music history. His influence can be heard in the works of his contemporaries, such as Haydn and Beethoven, as well as later composers.

Timeless Operas:

Mozart's operas remain some of the most beloved and frequently performed in the opera repertoire. Works like "The Marriage of Figaro," "Don Giovanni," and "The Magic Flute" continue to enchant audiences worldwide with their profound storytelling and exquisite music.

Relevance in Contemporary Culture:

Mozart's music continues to resonate with modern audiences, finding its way into popular culture through film, television, commercials, and adaptations in various musical genres.

Salzburg's Cultural Heritage:

Mozart's legacy is deeply interwoven with the cultural heritage of Salzburg. The city takes great pride in its association with the composer, celebrating his life and music through various events, museums, and landmarks dedicated to him.

Iconic Status:

Mozart's enduring popularity and iconic status have made him one of the most recognizable figures in classical music. His name and image are synonymous with artistic brilliance and musical genius.

Inspiration for Artists:

Mozart's compositions have been a profound source of inspiration for musicians, artists, and performers across generations. His music continues to be studied, interpreted, and performed by countless musicians worldwide.

Immortalized in Literature and Film:

Mozart's life and music have been the subject of numerous books, plays, and films, reflecting the fascination that his genius and personality continue to evoke.

Universal Appeal:

Mozart's music transcends cultural and geographical boundaries, appealing to people of all ages and backgrounds. His compositions have a universal quality that touches the human spirit.

Salzburg Festival

The Salzburg Festival is one of the most prestigious and renowned music and performing arts festivals in the world. It takes place annually in Salzburg, Austria, and is dedicated to celebrating the arts in all their forms. The festival was founded in 1920 by theater director Max Reinhardt, composer Richard Strauss, poet Hugo von Hofmannsthal, and conductor Franz Schalk, with the aim of reviving the cultural life of Salzburg after World War I. Since its inception, the Salzburg Festival has become a cultural highlight, attracting artists, musicians, and audiences from around the globe. Key Features of the Salzburg Festival:

Dates and Duration:

The Salzburg Festival is held every year from late July to late August. It spans for about five to six weeks, during which time the city of Salzburg becomes a hub of artistic activity.

Venue:

The festival utilizes various venues across Salzburg, including the iconic Grosses Festspielhaus (Great Festival Hall), the Haus für Mozart (House for Mozart), the Felsenreitschule (Rock Riding School), and the Salzburg Cathedral, among others. These venues provide stunning settings for concerts, opera performances, theater productions, and more.

Music and Opera Performances:

The festival showcases a diverse range of music genres, including orchestral concerts, chamber music, recitals, and opera performances. It features some of the world's finest musicians, conductors, and singers.

Opera Productions:

The Salzburg Festival is particularly renowned for its opera productions. World-class opera singers and directors stage extraordinary performances of classic operas and contemporary works.

Theater and Drama:

In addition to music, the festival features theater and drama performances, presenting a variety of theatrical works from classic plays to modern productions.

Salzburg Marionette Theater:

The Salzburg Marionette Theater, founded in 1913, is an integral part of the festival, staging puppet theater performances of classic operas and fairy tales.

Contemporary Art and Culture:

The festival often incorporates contemporary art and cultural events, exploring new artistic trends and experimental works.

Cultural Events and Exhibitions:

Outside of the performances, the festival hosts a range of cultural events, including exhibitions, talks, and panel discussions, providing a platform for dialogue and artistic exchange.

International Audience:

The Salzburg Festival attracts a diverse international audience, making it a melting pot of cultures and a hub for artistic appreciation.

Salzburg Cultural Heritage:

The festival contributes significantly to Salzburg's cultural heritage, celebrating its rich history and association with great artists and musicians.

Salzburg Marionette Theater

The Salzburg Marionette Theater is one of the oldest and most renowned puppet theaters in the world. Founded in 1913 by Anton Aicher, it has a rich history of presenting captivating puppetry performances, particularly of classic operas and fairy tales. The theater is located in the heart of Salzburg's Old Town and is an integral part of the city's cultural heritage and artistic identity. Here are some key features of the Salzburg Marionette Theater:

Puppet Theater Tradition:

The Salzburg Marionette Theater has a long tradition of producing high-quality puppet theater performances. Its unique art form combines the skillful manipulation of marionettes with storytelling, music, and set design.

Classic Operas and Fairy Tales:

The theater is renowned for its interpretations of classic operas by composers such as Mozart, Wagner, Verdi, and more. Performances often include popular operas like "The Magic Flute," "Carmen," "The Marriage of Figaro," and "Don Giovanni," among others.

Authentic Productions:

The Salzburg Marionette Theater stays true to the original librettos and music of the operas it performs, allowing audiences to experience these timeless classics in an authentic and innovative way.

Elaborate Sets and Costumes:

The theater's productions feature meticulously crafted sets and intricately designed marionettes, which bring the stories to life with astonishing detail.

Live Music Accompaniment:

Performances at the Salzburg Marionette Theater are accompanied by live music, further enhancing the emotional impact of the shows.

Family-Friendly Performances:

The theater caters to audiences of all ages, making it a family-friendly destination. Children and adults alike can enjoy the enchanting performances and captivating storytelling.

International Recognition:

The Salzburg Marionette Theater has earned international acclaim and has performed in numerous countries, furthering the art of puppetry on a global stage.

Time-Honored Tradition:

The art of puppetry is deeply ingrained in Salzburg's cultural heritage, and the theater's performances honor this time-honored tradition.

Modern Interpretations:

While the theater remains committed to preserving traditional puppetry techniques, it also presents modern interpretations of classic works, keeping the art form relevant and engaging for contemporary audiences.

Salzburg Cultural Experience:

A visit to the Salzburg Marionette Theater provides a unique and immersive cultural experience, allowing visitors to appreciate the artistry and creativity of puppetry.

Classical Music Scene

Salzburg's classical music scene is vibrant, steeped in history, and renowned worldwide. The city's deep musical heritage, including its association with Wolfgang Amadeus Mozart, has contributed to its reputation as a hub for classical music enthusiasts. Here are some key aspects of Salzburg's classical music scene:

Salzburg Festival:

The Salzburg Festival, held annually from late July to late August, is one of the most prestigious classical music events in the world. It attracts top musicians, conductors, and opera singers, who perform in the city's stunning venues, including the Grosses Festspielhaus and the Haus für Mozart.

Classical Concerts:

Throughout the year, Salzburg hosts a plethora of classical concerts featuring local and international orchestras, ensembles, and soloists. Venues like the Mozarteum, Mirabell Palace, and St. Peter's Abbey are known for their exceptional classical music performances.

Mozart Week:

Mozart Week is an annual music festival held in January to celebrate the birthday of Wolfgang Amadeus Mozart. It features a series of concerts and performances dedicated to the composer's works.

Mozarteum University of Salzburg:

The Mozarteum University of Salzburg is a renowned music conservatory that attracts talented musicians and offers a wide range of music programs, contributing to the city's vibrant music scene.

Salzburg Marionette Theater:

The Salzburg Marionette Theater is an integral part of the city's cultural landscape, offering puppet theater performances of classic operas and works.

Chamber Music:

Salzburg hosts numerous chamber music concerts, offering intimate performances in historic venues, allowing audiences to experience classical music up close.

St. Peter's Abbey Concert Series:

St. Peter's Abbey, one of Salzburg's historic landmarks, hosts a concert series featuring chamber music, choral performances, and organ recitals.

Salzburg Cultural Institutions:

Salzburg is home to cultural institutions that promote classical music, including the Salzburg Cultural Association and the International Mozarteum Foundation.

Youth Music Education:

The city emphasizes music education for young musicians, with various youth orchestras, choirs, and music schools nurturing the talents of the next generation of classical musicians.

Sound of Salzburg Show:

For visitors looking for a blend of classical and folk music, the Sound of Salzburg Show offers performances of traditional Austrian music and Mozart's compositions.

Traditional Folk Music

Traditional folk music is an integral part of Austria's cultural heritage, including Salzburg. Rooted in centuries-old traditions, Austrian folk music reflects the country's diverse history, landscape, and cultural influences. Here are some key features of traditional folk music in Salzburg:

Local Instruments:

Traditional Austrian folk music often features unique and traditional instruments, such as the zither, an Alpine harp-like instrument, and the Styrian accordion (Steirische Harmonika). The yodeling, a form of singing with rapid changes between chest and head voice, is also a characteristic element of folk music.

Alpine Folk Music:

Salzburg's folk music is heavily influenced by the Alpine region. Alpine folk music includes lively polkas, waltzes, and Ländlers, which are traditional Austrian folk dances.

Folk Songs and Lyrics:

Folk songs often tell stories of local history, nature, love, and everyday life. The lyrics are often sung in dialect, showcasing regional linguistic characteristics.

Schuhplattler Dance:

The Schuhplattler is a traditional dance form in Austria that involves slapping the thighs, knees, and soles of the shoes in a rhythmic pattern. It is often performed in traditional costumes during folk festivals and cultural events.

Folk Festivals and Events:

Salzburg hosts numerous folk festivals and events throughout the year, celebrating the region's musical heritage. These events feature traditional music, dances, and costume displays.

Folk Ensembles:

Folk music ensembles and groups, often consisting of locals, keep the traditions alive by performing at events and preserving the art of folk music.

Cultural Significance:

Traditional folk music plays an essential role in Austrian culture, fostering a sense of identity and pride among the locals. It also brings communities together during festivals and social gatherings.

Folk Music and Tourism:

Traditional folk music is an important part of Salzburg's tourism industry, with visitors seeking authentic cultural experiences by attending folk music performances and festivals.

Integration into Modern Music:

While traditional folk music remains an essential part of Salzburg's cultural heritage, it has also influenced contemporary Austrian music, and elements of folk music can be found in various genres.

Folk Music Education:

Austria places emphasis on preserving traditional folk music, and folk music education is offered in music schools and conservatories, ensuring that the tradition is passed on to future generations.

Architecture and History

Salzburg's architecture and history are deeply intertwined, creating a captivating tapestry of heritage that reflects the city's rich past and cultural significance. The city's architectural marvels, with their Baroque and Gothic elements, stand as testaments to Salzburg's historical prominence and artistic legacy. Here are some key features of Salzburg's architecture and history:

Baroque Architecture:

Salzburg is renowned for its Baroque architecture, which flourished during the rule of the Prince-Archbishops in the 17th and 18th centuries. Grand buildings, palaces, and churches, adorned with elaborate facades, stucco work, and frescoes, exemplify the opulence and artistic expression of the Baroque era.

Mirabell Palace:

Mirabell Palace is a splendid example of Baroque architecture. Its stunning gardens and majestic staircase have made it a favorite spot for visitors and a UNESCO World Heritage Site.

Hohensalzburg Fortress:

Perched high above the city, Hohensalzburg Fortress is one of the largest fully preserved medieval fortresses in Europe. Its towering presence and strategic location offer breathtaking views of Salzburg's Old Town and the surrounding landscape.

Salzburg Cathedral (Salzburger Dom):

The Salzburg Cathedral is a masterpiece of Baroque and Romanesque architecture. Its majestic facade, impressive dome, and lavish interior reflect the city's historical and religious significance.

Getreidegasse:

Getreidegasse is a charming street in Salzburg's Old Town known for its narrow, medieval architecture. It is famous as the birthplace of Wolfgang Amadeus Mozart.

Salzburg Residenz:

The Salzburg Residenz, the former residence of the Prince-Archbishops, showcases opulent rooms, elegant ballrooms, and exquisite architecture.

St. Peter's Abbey and Cemetery:

St. Peter's Abbey, founded in the 7th century, is one of the oldest monasteries in the German-speaking world. The abbey and its cemetery are notable for their historical and cultural significance.

Festungsgasse and Judengasse:

These ancient streets in the Old Town are filled with charming architecture, quaint shops, and historical landmarks.

Romanesque Architecture:

Romanesque architecture can be seen in some of Salzburg's oldest churches, such as St. Peter's Church, with its striking facade and ancient crypts.

UNESCO World Heritage Site:

Salzburg's historic city center, with its well-preserved architectural ensemble, was designated a UNESCO World Heritage Site in 1996, recognizing its cultural value and significance.

Museums and Galleries

Salzburg is home to a diverse range of museums and galleries, each offering a unique perspective on the city's rich history, art, and cultural heritage. From historical landmarks to contemporary art spaces, these institutions provide an immersive and enriching experience for visitors. Here are some key museums and galleries in Salzburg:

Mozart's Birthplace (Mozarts Geburtshaus):

This museum is dedicated to the life and works of Wolfgang Amadeus Mozart and is located in the house where the famous composer was born. It showcases Mozart's personal belongings, musical instruments, and original manuscripts.

Mozart's Residence (Mozarts Wohnhaus):

Mozart's Residence is another museum dedicated to the composer's life. It offers insight into Mozart's later years in Salzburg and features exhibits about his family and musical career.

Salzburg Museum:

The Salzburg Museum is a comprehensive museum showcasing the history and cultural heritage of the city and the region. It features exhibits on archaeology, art, and Salzburg's historical development.

Residenzgalerie Salzburg:

The Residenzgalerie is an art gallery located in the Salzburg Residenz, showcasing a remarkable collection of European paintings from the 16th to the 19th century.

Modern Art Oxford at The Yard:

This contemporary art space in Salzburg presents rotating exhibitions of modern and contemporary art, providing a platform for local and international artists.

Panorama Museum Salzburg:

The Panorama Museum houses the famous Panorama of the City of Salzburg, a circular painting that offers a panoramic view of the city in the 19th century.

Museum der Moderne Salzburg (Museum of Modern Art):

Located on the Mönchsberg, this museum features modern and contemporary art, including paintings, sculptures, and multimedia installations.

Salzburg Marionette Theater:

While not a traditional museum, the Salzburg Marionette Theater showcases a unique art form of puppetry, presenting classic operas and fairy tales with marionettes.

Stiegl-Brauwelt (Stiegl World of Beer):

This interactive museum offers insights into the history of beer brewing in Salzburg and includes beer tastings and exhibits on beer production.

DomQuartier Salzburg:

The DomQuartier is a unique museum complex that combines the Salzburg Cathedral, the Residenz, the Dom Museum, and the St. Peter's Museum. It offers a comprehensive cultural experience.

Cultural Events and Festivals

Salzburg is a city rich in cultural events and festivals, offering a vibrant calendar of celebrations that reflect its artistic heritage and love for music, theater, and the arts. From world-renowned music festivals to traditional folk events, Salzburg hosts a diverse array of cultural happenings throughout the year. Here are some key cultural events and festivals in Salzburg:

Salzburg Festival:

The Salzburg Festival is one of the world's most prestigious music and performing arts festivals. Held annually from late July to late August, it features opera performances, classical concerts, theater productions, and more. Renowned artists from around the world come to Salzburg to showcase their talents, making it a cultural highlight of the year.

Mozart Week (Mozartwoche):

Mozart Week is an annual music festival held in late January to celebrate the birthday of Wolfgang Amadeus Mozart. It features a series of concerts, recitals, and opera performances dedicated to the composer's works.

Salzburg Easter Festival:

The Salzburg Easter Festival, founded by Herbert von Karajan, takes place around Easter and features opera and classical music performances. It is known for its high-quality productions and esteemed artists.

Salzburg Advent Singing:

During the Advent season, Salzburg comes alive with festive Christmas markets and musical events, including the Salzburg Advent Singing. This tradition features choirs, folk music groups, and Christmas carols.

Salzburg Whitsun Festival:

The Salzburg Whitsun Festival is a music festival held during the Pentecost weekend. It features concerts, opera performances, and chamber music by acclaimed artists.

Festungskonzerte (Fortress Concerts):

During the summer months, the Hohensalzburg Fortress hosts a series of concerts, showcasing classical music in a historical setting with panoramic views of the city.

St. Rupert's Fair (Ruperti-Kirtag):

St. Rupert's Fair is an annual traditional folk festival held in honor of the city's patron saint, St. Rupert. It features traditional music, dance, food, and local crafts.

Pantomime Festival:

The Pantomime Festival brings together international pantomime artists and performers, celebrating the art of silent storytelling and physical theater.

Salzburg Cultural Days (Salzburger Kulturtage):

This festival celebrates the diversity of Salzburg's cultural scene, featuring various art forms, including music, theater, dance, and visual arts.

Lake Festival (Salzburger Festspiele am Domplatz):

During the Salzburg Festival, the famous Domplatz hosts open-air performances and concerts, providing an atmospheric and unique cultural experience.

Salzburg's Cultural Heritage Sites

Salzburg's cultural heritage sites are a testament to the city's rich history, architectural splendor, and artistic legacy. From grand palaces and churches to well-preserved medieval streets, these sites provide an immersive journey through Salzburg's cultural heritage. Here are some of the city's most notable cultural heritage sites:

Salzburg Old Town (Altstadt):

Salzburg's Old Town is a UNESCO World Heritage Site and a treasure trove of historical landmarks. Its charming medieval streets, Baroque architecture, and well-preserved buildings reflect the city's past as a prosperous cultural center.

Hohensalzburg Fortress:

Perched on a hill overlooking the city, Hohensalzburg Fortress is one of the largest and best-preserved medieval fortresses in Europe. It offers breathtaking views and a glimpse into the city's medieval history.

Mirabell Palace and Gardens:

Mirabell Palace is a stunning Baroque masterpiece surrounded by manicured gardens. The Marble Hall inside the palace is famous for its exquisite architecture and historical significance.

Salzburg Cathedral (Salzburger Dom):

A masterpiece of Baroque and Romanesque architecture, the Salzburg Cathedral is a symbol of the city's religious and cultural heritage.

St. Peter's Abbey and Cemetery:

St. Peter's Abbey, founded in the 7th century, is one of the oldest monasteries in the German-speaking world. Its cemetery is the final resting place of several notable personalities, including Mozart's sister Nannerl.

Nonnberg Abbey:

Founded in the 8th century, Nonnberg Abbey is one of the oldest continuously inhabited convents in the world. It holds historical and religious significance and is featured in "The Sound of Music."

Mozarts Geburtshaus (Mozart's Birthplace):

The house where Wolfgang Amadeus Mozart was born is now a museum dedicated to the composer's life and works. It provides an intimate glimpse into his early years and musical journey.

Mozarts Wohnhaus (Mozart's Residence):

Mozart's Residence offers insights into the composer's later years in Salzburg and features exhibits on his family and musical career.

Salzburg Residenz:

The Salzburg Residenz served as the palace of the Prince-Archbishops and is a testament to the city's historical prominence. Its opulent rooms and ballrooms are a feast for the eyes.

Getreidegasse:

Getreidegasse is a charming medieval street in the Old Town, known for its narrow passageways, traditional shop signs, and historical significance as the birthplace of Mozart.

CUISINE AND CULINARY DELIGHTS

Salzburg's cuisine is a delightful blend of traditional Austrian dishes, hearty alpine flavors, and international influences. From savory comfort foods to delectable desserts, the city's culinary scene offers a diverse range of flavors to satisfy every palate.

Salzburg Cuisine

Schnitzel:

Austrian schnitzel is a beloved dish in Salzburg and across the country. It consists of breaded and fried veal or pork cutlets, served with a slice of lemon and often accompanied by potato salad or parsley potatoes.

Salzburger Nockerl:

A famous Salzburg specialty, Salzburger Nockerl is a fluffy soufflé-like dessert made with egg whites, sugar, and vanilla, sprinkled with powdered sugar, and often served with fruit compote.

Kasnocken:

Kasnocken is a hearty alpine dish made of small dumplings mixed with melted cheese and topped with fried onions. It is a comforting and satisfying meal, perfect for colder days.

Salzburger Bier:

Salzburg is home to several local breweries, and trying the city's beer is a must. Sip on a refreshing pint of Salzburger Stiegl beer, a popular choice among locals.

Mozartkugel:

The Mozartkugel is a famous chocolate praline named after Wolfgang Amadeus Mozart. It consists of a marzipan core, nougat, and dark chocolate, and is a sweet treat to bring home as a souvenir.

Tafelspitz:

Tafelspitz is a classic Austrian dish of boiled beef served with a variety of traditional side dishes, such as roasted potatoes, creamed spinach, and horseradish sauce.

Apple Strudel:

This Austrian classic is a must-try dessert. Apple strudel features thin layers of flaky pastry filled with cinnamon-spiced apples and served with a dollop of whipped cream.

Dumplings (Knödel):

Austrian cuisine is famous for its various types of dumplings, including bread dumplings, potato dumplings, and semolina dumplings, which are often served as side dishes with meat or stew.

Goulash:

Goulash, a hearty meat stew seasoned with paprika and other spices, is a popular dish in Austria. It is often served with dumplings or potatoes.

Alpine Cheeses:

Salzburg's proximity to the Alps ensures a rich variety of high-quality alpine cheeses. Don't miss the opportunity to try local cheeses, such as Bergkäse and Almkäse.

Coffeehouse Culture

Salzburg's coffeehouse culture is an integral part of the city's social fabric, offering a relaxed and welcoming environment for locals and visitors alike. Rooted in a long tradition of coffee consumption, Salzburg's coffeehouses have become iconic institutions that celebrate the art of coffee brewing and the pleasure of spending time in good company. Here are some key aspects of Salzburg's coffeehouse culture:

Historic Coffeehouses:

Many of Salzburg's coffeehouses have a storied history, dating back several centuries. These establishments have preserved their traditional charm and offer an authentic glimpse into the city's coffeehouse culture.

Coffeehouse Interiors:

Salzburg's coffeehouses boast elegant and cozy interiors, often adorned with classic furniture, chandeliers, and ornate decorations. The atmosphere invites guests to linger and savor their coffee.

Kaffee und Kuchen (Coffee and Cake):

One of the quintessential traditions of Salzburg's coffeehouse culture is "Kaffee und Kuchen," which translates to "coffee and cake." Locals and visitors enjoy pairing their coffee with a delectable selection of homemade cakes, pastries, and desserts.

Traditional Coffee Varieties:

Salzburg's coffeehouses offer a wide range of coffee varieties, including the classic "Verlängerter" (a milder version of a coffee with extra hot water), "Melange" (similar to a cappuccino), and "Kleiner Brauner" (espresso with a dash of milk).

Time to Relax and Socialize:

The coffeehouse culture in Salzburg encourages guests to take their time and enjoy their coffee while engaging in conversation, reading a newspaper, or simply people-watching.

Coffeehouse Literature:

Salzburg's coffeehouses have been a gathering place for artists, writers, and intellectuals throughout history. Many famous literary figures have found inspiration and companionship in the city's coffeehouses.

Coffeehouse Music:

Some coffeehouses in Salzburg host live music performances, adding to the delightful ambiance and cultural experience.

Historic Coffeehouse Names:

Many of the coffeehouses in Salzburg have interesting and unique names, reflecting their historical significance and character.

Salzburg's Coffeehouse Heritage:

Salzburg's coffeehouse culture has been recognized as part of the city's intangible cultural heritage, further underscoring its importance in the local community.

A Part of Daily Life:

For locals, visiting a coffeehouse is more than just having a cup of coffee; it is a cherished daily ritual that fosters a sense of belonging and community.

Best Restaurants

Salzburg is home to a diverse culinary scene with a wide range of restaurants offering delicious dishes and a delightful dining experience. Here are some of the best restaurants in Salzburg that cater to different tastes and preferences:

Restaurant IMLAUER Sky Bar & Restaurant:

Located at the top of the IMLAUER Hotel Pitter Salzburg, this rooftop restaurant offers stunning panoramic views of the city along with a diverse menu of Austrian and international cuisine.

St. Peter Stiftskeller:

Set in one of the oldest restaurants in Europe, dating back to 803 AD, St. Peter Stiftskeller offers a historical and elegant dining experience with a menu featuring Austrian specialties.

Zum Zirkelwirt:

A family-run restaurant since 1411, Zum Zirkelwirt serves traditional Austrian dishes with a focus on local and organic ingredients.

Esszimmer:

For a fine dining experience, Esszimmer is a Michelin-starred restaurant offering innovative and creative cuisine with carefully curated wine pairings.

Gasthof Goldgasse:

This charming restaurant in the heart of the Old Town serves modern Austrian cuisine with an emphasis on regional and seasonal ingredients.

M32 Panorama Restaurant:

Located at the Museum der Moderne on the Mönchsberg, M32 offers breathtaking views of Salzburg's Old Town and a menu inspired by Mediterranean and Austrian flavors.

Carpe Diem Finest Fingerfood:

Carpe Diem is renowned for its creative finger food and contemporary cuisine. The restaurant's stylish ambiance and culinary delights make it a popular choice.

Restaurant Esszimmer M32:

Set in the historic Mönchsberg cliffside, this elegant restaurant offers modern and imaginative cuisine with an emphasis on local and organic ingredients.

Triangel:

Triangel is a cozy bistro serving authentic Austrian dishes and local specialties, making it a favorite among both locals and visitors.

K+K Restaurant am Waagplatz:

Located in a historic building, K+K Restaurant am Waagplatz offers Austrian cuisine with a modern twist, along with a selection of international dishes.

NATURE ESCAPES

Salzburg offers a wide range of nature escapes for those seeking outdoor adventures and a retreat into nature's beauty. From picturesque alpine landscapes to serene lakes and nature reserves, the region provides ample opportunities for hiking, biking, and relaxing in the great outdoors. Here are some nature escapes in and around Salzburg:

Salzburg's Lakes

Salzburg is surrounded by a picturesque region known as the Salzkammergut, which is home to several stunning lakes. Each lake offers its own unique charm and opportunities for outdoor activities, making them popular destinations for both locals and tourists. Here are some of the notable lakes near Salzburg:

Wolfgangsee:

Located about 45 minutes from Salzburg, Wolfgangsee is one of the most scenic lakes in the region. Surrounded by mountains, the lake offers opportunities for swimming, boating, and scenic walks along its shores. The towns of St.

Wolfgang, Strobl, and St. Gilgen, situated along the lake, add to its picturesque appeal.

Fuschlsee:

Fuschlsee is another beautiful lake in the Salzkammergut region, known for its crystal-clear waters and lush surroundings. It offers swimming, boating, and hiking opportunities, and the village of Fuschl am See on its shores is a charming spot to explore.

Mondsee:

Mondsee is a larger lake with a unique shape, and it is famous for its role as the backdrop for the wedding scene in the movie "The Sound of Music." The town of Mondsee, with its historic church and quaint streets, adds to the lake's allure.

Wallersee:

Located to the north of Salzburg, Wallersee is a popular lake for water sports and fishing. Its sandy beaches and gentle waters make it a family-friendly destination.

Mattsee:

Situated close to Wallersee, Mattsee is a peaceful lake with a small island hosting a historic castle and monastery. It's a great spot for relaxation and leisurely walks.

Zeller See:

Although slightly farther from Salzburg, Zeller See is a larger lake known for its recreational activities, such as swimming, sailing, and fishing. The charming town of Zell am See offers a range of dining and shopping options.

Hintersee:

Hintersee is a smaller lake surrounded by dense forests and majestic mountains, making it a favorite spot for nature lovers and photographers.

Hallstätter See:

Hallstätter See, a bit further from Salzburg, is one of the most famous and picturesque lakes in Austria. The idyllic village of Hallstatt on its shores is a UNESCO World Heritage Site and attracts visitors from around the world.

Salzburg Mountains and Hills

Salzburg is surrounded by a beautiful landscape of mountains and hills, making it an ideal destination for outdoor enthusiasts and nature lovers. The city's proximity to the Alps and its location in the Salzburg basin offer a diverse range of hiking trails, scenic viewpoints, and opportunities for outdoor activities. Here are some of the notable mountains and hills near Salzburg:

Untersberg:

The Untersberg is one of the most iconic mountains near Salzburg, offering breathtaking panoramic views of the city and the surrounding countryside. It is easily accessible by a cable car and offers various hiking routes suitable for different fitness levels.

Gaisberg:

Gaisberg is a popular mountain located just a short distance from Salzburg's city center. It is a favored spot for hiking, mountain biking, and paragliding, with several well-marked trails leading to its summit.

Kapuzinerberg:

Kapuzinerberg is a hill located within Salzburg's city limits, providing excellent hiking trails and beautiful views of the city and the surrounding landscape.

Tennengebirge:

Tennengebirge is a picturesque mountain range offering various hiking trails and opportunities for nature exploration.

Mönchsberg:

Mönchsberg is another city hill offering scenic walking paths and viewpoints. It is home to the Museum der Moderne Salzburg, providing a perfect blend of culture and nature.

Dachstein Mountains:

The Dachstein Mountains, a bit farther from Salzburg, are a stunning alpine range offering opportunities for hiking, climbing, and enjoying the beauty of the Austrian Alps.

Hoher Göll:

Hoher Göll is a prominent peak in the Berchtesgaden Alps, providing challenging hiking routes and magnificent views of the surrounding mountains.

Nockstein:

Nockstein is a small hill near Salzburg, offering scenic walking paths and panoramic views of the city.

Watzmann:

Watzmann, located in the Berchtesgaden Alps, is one of the most famous peaks in the region, attracting hikers and climbers from around the world.

Osterhorn Mountains:

The Osterhorn Mountains offer a tranquil landscape with hiking trails that lead through lush meadows and dense forests.

Parks and Gardens

Salzburg boasts a variety of parks and gardens that offer serene escapes from the bustling city, providing a tranquil environment to relax, stroll, and enjoy nature. These green spaces offer an array of beautifully landscaped gardens, historic landmarks, and scenic spots for both locals and visitors to explore. Here are some of the notable parks and gardens in Salzburg:

Mirabell Gardens (Mirabellgarten):

The Mirabell Gardens, located next to Mirabell Palace, are among the most famous in Salzburg. The beautifully manicured gardens feature ornate flowerbeds, statues, fountains, and geometrically arranged hedges, creating a charming and elegant ambiance. The gardens are often associated with scenes from "The Sound of Music" and are a popular spot for visitors to wander and enjoy the surroundings.

Hellbrunn Palace and Gardens:

The gardens of Hellbrunn Palace, with their playful trick fountains, are a unique and entertaining experience. The beautifully landscaped grounds provide a picturesque backdrop for leisurely walks and exploration. The palace itself is a historical and architectural gem.

Volksgarten:

Volksgarten, or the People's Garden, is a public park located near the Salzburg Residenz. It features well-maintained flowerbeds, walking paths, and an ornate rose garden that bursts with color during the summer months.

Mirabell Palace Dwarf Garden (Zwerglgarten):

Adjacent to the Mirabell Gardens, the Dwarf Garden is a delightful display of humorous dwarf statues and whimsical sculptures. It adds a touch of charm and playfulness to the overall beauty of the palace grounds.

Kapitelplatz:

Kapitelplatz is a public square located in the heart of the Old Town. While not a traditional garden, it features the famous Sphaera, a large golden sphere designed by Stephan Balkenhol, which is a popular meeting point and photo spot.

Salzburg City Park (Stadtpark):

Salzburg City Park is a green oasis in the city center, providing ample space for picnics, leisurely walks, and relaxation. The park is home to the famous statue of Wolfgang Amadeus Mozart.

Aigen Park:

Aigen Park, located in the Aigen neighborhood, offers a peaceful setting with large lawns, meandering paths, and a small lake. It's a perfect spot for a quiet escape and nature appreciation.

Mirabell Palace Hedge Theater (Heckentheater):

The Hedge Theater, located within the Mirabell Gardens, features rows of meticulously trimmed hedges forming a natural amphitheater, providing a unique space for outdoor performances and events.

Gaisberg Park:

Gaisberg Park offers sweeping views of Salzburg and the surrounding countryside. It's a great spot for panoramic vistas and enjoying the fresh mountain air.

Freisaal Garden:

Located on the outskirts of Salzburg, Freisaal Garden is a beautiful, well-maintained park that provides a tranquil atmosphere away from the city's hustle and bustle.

Almkanal

The Almkanal is a scenic canal that runs through Salzburg, offering pleasant walking and biking paths along its banks.

Salzach River

The Salzach River runs through the center of Salzburg, dividing the city into two parts, the Altstadt (Old Town) on the left bank and the Neustadt (New Town) on the right bank. Several bridges connect the two sides, including the iconic Makartsteg and Mozartsteg pedestrian bridges, which offer stunning views of the river and the city's historic architecture. The riverside promenades on both banks provide scenic walking and biking paths, where locals and visitors alike can enjoy a leisurely stroll and admire the city's landmarks from the water's edge.

Rivers

Salzburg is characterized by the presence of the Salzach River, which runs through the heart of the city and divides it into two distinct parts: the Altstadt (Old Town) and the Neustadt (New Town). The Salzach River is not only a significant geographical feature but also an integral part of Salzburg's cultural and historical identity. Here are some key aspects of the Salzach River in Salzburg:

Geographical Significance:

The Salzach River is one of the main rivers in Austria, originating in the state of Salzburg and flowing through several regions before eventually joining the Inn River in the city of Passau, Germany.

Dividing the City:

The river divides Salzburg into the left bank (Altstadt) and right bank (Neustadt). The historic Old Town, with its medieval charm and cultural landmarks, lies on the left bank, while the modern New Town features more contemporary architecture and residential areas on the right bank.

Bridges:

Several bridges span the Salzach River, providing essential connections between the two sides of the city. Some of the most notable bridges include the Makartsteg, Mozartsteg, Staatsbrücke, and Müllnersteg. These bridges are not only functional but also architectural landmarks, offering fantastic views of the river and surrounding scenery.

Scenic Beauty:

The Salzach River enhances Salzburg's picturesque landscape, providing a stunning backdrop to the city's historical buildings, lush parks, and rolling hills.

Waterfront Promenades:

The riverbanks on both sides feature scenic promenades that offer fantastic opportunities for walking, jogging, cycling, or simply enjoying the peaceful atmosphere along the water.

Cultural Heritage:

The Salzach River has played a crucial role in Salzburg's cultural and economic development. It was a significant trade route in the past and contributed to the city's prosperity.

Boat Tours and Cruises:

Boat tours and cruises along the Salzach River are popular activities for tourists. These trips offer unique perspectives of Salzburg's landmarks, including the Hohensalzburg Fortress and the picturesque cityscape.

Relaxation and Recreation:

The Salzach River is not only a sightseeing attraction but also a place for locals and visitors to relax and enjoy nature. Many choose to have a leisurely picnic or simply sit by the riverbanks and unwind.

Gorges

Salzburg and its surrounding region offer several stunning gorges, each providing a unique and captivating natural experience. Gorges are narrow, steep-sided valleys carved by water, and they offer opportunities for hiking, sightseeing, and admiring the beauty of nature. Here are some of the notable gorges near Salzburg:

Lammerklamm Gorge:

The Lammerklamm Gorge, also located near Golling, offers a striking walking trail with wooden walkways along the riverbed. The gorge's dramatic walls and the rushing waters of the Lammer River create a picturesque setting for a nature walk.

Taugl Gorge (Tauglbachklamm):

The Taugl Gorge is a hidden gem located near Hallein, around 20 kilometers south of Salzburg. A well-maintained hiking trail leads through the gorge, which features waterfalls, natural pools, and moss-covered cliffs.

Strubklamm Gorge:

The Strubklamm Gorge is situated near the village of St. Martin am Tennengebirge, approximately 60 kilometers south of Salzburg. The gorge offers a delightful hiking path through lush forests and along the Strubklamm River.

Leopoldskroner Moor:

Leopoldskroner Moor is a picturesque moorland located near the Leopoldskron Palace, famous for its appearance in "The Sound of Music." The moor features wooden walkways, ponds, and diverse wildlife.

Seisenbergklamm Gorge:

Although slightly farther from Salzburg, the Seisenbergklamm Gorge is worth the visit. It is located near the village of Weißbach bei Lofer, approximately 60 kilometers southwest of Salzburg. The gorge offers a spectacular trail with bridges and viewing platforms, allowing visitors to admire the steep rock walls and the roaring river.

Vorderkaserklamm and Hinterssee Gorge:

Located near St. Martin bei Lofer, these two gorges offer a combination of natural beauty, waterfalls, and clear alpine waters.

Tennen Mountains:

The Tennen Mountains, located southwest of Salzburg, offer various gorges and stunning natural landscapes. These include the Kuchlerklamm and the Guggenbichlklamm, both providing scenic hiking routes.

Waterfalls

Salzburg and its surrounding region boast several picturesque waterfalls, each offering a mesmerizing display of nature's power and beauty. These cascading waterfalls are popular destinations for nature enthusiasts, hikers, and those seeking a refreshing escape. Here are some of the notable waterfalls near Salzburg:

Golling Waterfall (Gollinger Wasserfall):

Located in the town of Golling, approximately 30 kilometers south of Salzburg, the Golling Waterfall is one of the region's most famous natural attractions. The waterfall drops 75 meters into a deep gorge, creating a stunning sight and a serene atmosphere. A short hike leads to viewpoints where visitors can enjoy the falls up close.

Krimml Waterfalls (Krimmler Wasserfälle):

The Krimml Waterfalls, situated about 80 kilometers southwest of Salzburg, are among the highest waterfalls in Europe. They cascade down in three stages with a total height of 380 meters. A hiking path allows visitors to explore the falls from different angles and enjoy spectacular views of the surrounding scenery.

Seisenbergklamm and Vorderkaserklamm Gorges:

Although not traditional waterfalls, the Seisenbergklamm and Vorderkaserklamm Gorges near St. Martin bei Lofer, approximately 60 kilometers southwest of Salzburg, offer rushing rivers and beautiful cascades within their narrow rock formations. Wooden walkways allow visitors to walk through the gorges and admire the water's force.

Gastein Waterfalls (Gasteiner Wasserfälle):

The Gastein Valley, approximately 90 kilometers south of Salzburg, is home to several waterfalls, including the Bad Gastein Waterfall and the Gastein Ache Waterfall. The Bad

Gastein Waterfall is particularly striking, plunging dramatically into the heart of the town.

Strubklamm Waterfall (Strubklamm Wasserfall):

Located near the village of St. Martin am Tennengebirge, approximately 60 kilometers south of Salzburg, the Strubklamm Waterfall is part of the Strubklamm Gorge. A hike through the gorge leads to the waterfall, making it a rewarding nature adventure.

Schleier Waterfall (Schleier Wasserfall):

Situated in the Obersulzbach Valley in Hohe Tauern National Park, the Schleier Waterfall is a stunning natural wonder. It cascades from a height of over 120 meters, creating a breathtaking sight for those who embark on the hike to reach it.

Wildkar Waterfall (Wildkar Wasserfall):

Located in the Untersulzbach Valley in Hohe Tauern National Park, the Wildkar Waterfall is a pristine alpine waterfall surrounded by picturesque landscapes.

Kitzsteinhorn Glacier

Kitzsteinhorn is a glacier located near the town of Kaprun in the Austrian state of Salzburg. It is one of the most popular and well-known ski areas in the region and offers year-round skiing and snowboarding opportunities due to its glacier's high altitude. Key features of Kitzsteinhorn include:

Glacier Skiing:

Kitzsteinhorn is known for its glacier skiing, which allows visitors to enjoy snow sports even during the summer months. The glacier offers a wide range of slopes and trails suitable for skiers and snowboarders of all levels, from beginners to experts.

Kitzsteinhorn Gipfelwelt 3000:

At the summit of Kitzsteinhorn, there is a viewing platform called Gipfelwelt 3000 (Summit World 3000). From here, visitors can enjoy breathtaking panoramic views of the surrounding mountains, including the Hohe Tauern National Park, Austria's largest national park.

Ice Arena:

The Ice Arena at Kitzsteinhorn features various snow and ice-related activities, such as ice skating and tubing, providing fun options for families and non-skiers.

Gletscherjet 3:

Gletscherjet 3 is a modern gondola lift that takes visitors from the valley station in Kaprun to the glacier ski area quickly and comfortably.

Kaprun Reservoirs:

In addition to skiing, Kitzsteinhorn is known for its high-alpine reservoirs. The Mooserboden and Wasserfallboden reservoirs are accessible by a scenic mountain road and offer a chance to explore the impressive hydroelectric power plants and stunning alpine landscapes.

TRAVEL TIPS

Safety Tips

Safety is paramount when traveling, and it's essential to take precautions to ensure a smooth and secure trip. Here are some travel safety tips to keep in mind:

1. **Research Your Destination:** Before you travel, research your destination thoroughly. Familiarize yourself with local customs, laws, and potential safety concerns.

2. **Keep Important Documents Secure:** Carry essential documents like passports, visas, and travel insurance in a secure, waterproof bag or pouch. Consider making digital copies as a backup.

3. **Stay Aware of Your Surroundings:** Be alert and aware of your surroundings at all times, especially in crowded places and tourist areas.

4. **Use Trusted Transportation:** Opt for official taxis or reputable transportation services, especially at airports and train stations.

5. **Avoid Flashing Valuables:** Avoid displaying expensive jewelry, cameras, or electronic devices in public, as they may attract unwanted attention.

6. **Use Hotel Safes:** Store valuables, passports, and extra cash in the hotel safe when not needed.

7. **Carry a Minimal Amount of Cash:** Avoid carrying large amounts of cash. Use credit cards or withdraw money from ATMs as needed.

8. **Beware of Scams:** Be cautious of scams, such as overcharging for services or distraction techniques to steal belongings.

9. **Respect Local Customs:** Dress appropriately and respect local customs and traditions to avoid unintentional offense.

10. **Stay Informed:** Keep up-to-date with the latest travel advisories and safety alerts for your destination.

11. **Plan Safe Accommodation:** Choose reputable and well-reviewed accommodations in safe neighborhoods.

12. **Travel Insurance:** Purchase comprehensive travel insurance that covers medical emergencies, trip cancellations, and theft.

13. **Emergency Contacts:** Keep a list of emergency contacts, including local authorities and your country's embassy or consulate.

14. **Know the Emergency Numbers:** Familiarize yourself with the local emergency numbers for police, ambulance, and fire services.

15. **Avoid Risky Areas at Night:** Avoid poorly lit or unfamiliar areas at night, and travel in groups if possible.

Local Insights

Local insights are invaluable when traveling as they offer authentic perspectives and tips from residents who know the city best. Here are some local insights for exploring Salzburg:

16. **Hidden Cafés and Eateries:** Locals can recommend lesser-known cafés and eateries with the best coffee, pastries, and traditional Austrian cuisine.

17. **Off-the-Beaten-Path Attractions:** Ask locals about hidden gems and lesser-known attractions that may not be as crowded with tourists.

18. **Festivals and Events:** Get information on local festivals, cultural events, and concerts that may be happening during your visit.

19. **Nature Escapes:** Locals can suggest beautiful hiking trails, nature spots, and scenic viewpoints for breathtaking vistas.

20. **Public Transportation Tips:** Get insights on navigating public transportation, including bus and tram routes, to explore the city like a local.

21. **Best Times to Visit Popular Sites:** Learn about the best times to visit popular attractions to avoid crowds and make the most of your experience.

22. **Local Traditions and Customs:** Gain insight into local customs, traditions, and etiquette to show respect and immerse yourself in the culture.

23. **Shopping Recommendations:** Discover local shops and boutiques for authentic souvenirs, handmade crafts, and unique finds.

24. **Nightlife Hotspots:** Locals can suggest the best bars, pubs, and live music venues to experience Salzburg's vibrant nightlife.

25. **Safety Tips:** Seek advice from locals on staying safe and avoiding potential risks in the city.

Budget-Friendly Travel Tips

Traveling on a budget in Salzburg is possible with careful planning and smart choices. Here are some budget-friendly travel tips for exploring Salzburg without breaking the bank:

26. **Free Walking Tours:** Join free walking tours offered by local companies or volunteers to explore Salzburg's landmarks and get insightful information from knowledgeable guides.

27. **Salzburg Card:** Consider purchasing the Salzburg Card, which provides free access to many attractions, public transportation, and discounts on tours and events.

28. **Picnics and Street Food:** Save on dining expenses by enjoying picnics in parks or along the Salzach River and trying affordable street food options.

29. **Local Markets:** Shop for fresh produce and local specialties at the Salzburg Food Market (Schranne) for budget-friendly meals and snacks.

30. **Budget Accommodations:** Look for budget accommodations like hostels, guesthouses, or budget hotels in the city center or nearby neighborhoods.

31. **Free Attractions:** Take advantage of free attractions such as the Mirabell Gardens, Kapuzinerberg Hill, and the exterior of Hohensalzburg Fortress.

32. **DIY Sightseeing:** Explore the Old Town on your own with self-guided walking tours, using maps and online resources to navigate.

33. **Discount Cards and Apps:** Check for discount cards, coupons, or apps offering deals on food, attractions, and transportation.

34. **Affordable Local Transport:** Use public transportation or consider walking or biking to explore the city's sights.

35. **Free Events and Festivals:** Check the local event calendar for free concerts, festivals, and cultural events that you can attend without a charge.

36. **Affordable Day Trips:** Opt for budget-friendly day trips to nearby attractions, such as Lake Wolfgang (Wolfgangsee) or Hallein Salt Mine.

37. **Free Museums:** Take advantage of free entry days at certain museums and art galleries to explore Salzburg's cultural offerings.

38. **Tap Water:** Save on bottled water costs by refilling your bottle with tap water, which is safe to drink in Salzburg.

39. **BYO Lunch:** Pack your own lunch for day trips to avoid eating at expensive tourist spots.

Solo Travel Tips in Salzburg

Solo travel in Salzburg can be a rewarding and enriching experience. As a solo traveler, you have the freedom to explore the city at your own pace, immerse yourself in the local culture, and connect with other travelers and locals. Here are some tips for a successful solo trip to Salzburg:

40. **Stay in Central Accommodations:** Choose accommodations in the city center or near popular attractions for convenience and easy access to public transportation.

41. **Join Guided Tours:** Consider joining guided tours, walking tours, or group activities to meet other travelers and make new connections.

42. **Safety First:** As with any destination, practice basic safety precautions, such as staying in well-lit areas at night and keeping your belongings secure.

43. **Engage with Locals:** Interact with locals, ask for recommendations, and engage in conversations to get insights into the city's culture and traditions.

44. **Solo Dining:** Don't hesitate to dine alone; embrace the opportunity to savor the local cuisine at your own pace and discover new flavors.

45. **Be Open to New Experiences:** Embrace spontaneity and be open to trying new activities, attending local events, and exploring off-the-beaten-path spots.

46. **Use Public Transportation:** Utilize the city's public transportation system to move around easily and efficiently.

47. **Attend Cultural Events:** Experience Salzburg's vibrant cultural scene by attending concerts, art exhibitions, or theater performances.

48. **Take Advantage of Solo Time:** Use your solo time to reflect, journal, or simply enjoy the peaceful moments to yourself.

49. **Practice Self-Care:** Take breaks when needed, stay hydrated, and prioritize self-care to make the most of your solo journey.

50. **Trust Your Instincts:** Trust your instincts and intuition while making decisions and exploring the city.

ITINERARIES

Mozart Heritage Tour

- Visit Mozart's Birthplace and Residence.

- Explore the Mozartsplatz and Statue of Mozart.

- Attend a classical concert or opera performance at a renowned venue.

- Enjoy coffee and cake at a traditional café, such as Café Tomaselli.

Salzburg Old Town Walking Tour

- Explore the historic Old Town (Altstadt) and its charming narrow streets.

- Visit Salzburg Cathedral and St. Peter's Abbey.

- Cross the Mozartsteg Pedestrian Bridge for picturesque views.

- Discover the medieval Hohensalzburg Fortress and its museums.

Sound of Music Tour

- Visit locations from "The Sound of Music" movie, such as Mirabell Gardens and Residenzplatz.

- Tour the Nonnberg Abbey, where Maria von Trapp was a postulant.
- Explore Leopoldskron Palace and Hellbrunn Palace (Von Trapp Villa).
- Sing along to the film's famous songs at iconic spots.

Nature and Hiking Expedition

- Take the Mönchsbergbahn funicular to Mönchsberg hill for scenic views.
- Hike along the Mönchsberg trails or Gaisberg mountain.
- Visit the Mirabell Gardens for a relaxing stroll.
- Have a picnic by the Salzach River or in Stadtpark.

Salzburg by Night

- Take an evening stroll through the illuminated Old Town.
- Join a Salzburg night tour to learn about the city's ghostly legends.
- Enjoy a riverside dinner at a restaurant with a view.
- Attend a classical music concert or enjoy live music at a local pub.

Baroque and Art Lover's Delight

- Visit Salzburg Baroque Museum for a glimpse into the city's artistic past.

- Explore the Museum der Moderne for contemporary art exhibitions.

- Discover St. Peter's Abbey Museum's art and cultural treasures.

- Enjoy a coffee and cake break at Café Bazar while soaking in the ambiance.

Family Fun Day

- Take a horse-drawn carriage ride through the Old Town.

- Visit the Salzburg Zoo and Hellbrunn Zoo.

- Explore the Toy Museum for a nostalgic trip down memory lane.

- End the day with a boat ride on the Salzach River.

Salzburg Culinary Experience

- Start with a traditional Austrian breakfast at Café Tomaselli.

- Visit the Salzburg Food Market for local delicacies and produce.

- Enjoy lunch at a traditional beer garden, like Müllner Bräu.

- Try Austrian specialties for dinner at a local restaurant.

Musical Journey through Salzburg

- Attend a performance at the Salzburg Marionette Theater.

- Take a backstage tour at the Salzburg State Theatre.
- Explore the Mozarts Wohnhaus for insights into Mozart's life.
- End the day with a musical walking tour through the city.

Day Trip to the Lakes and Mountains

- Visit Lake Wolfgang (Wolfgangsee) for a scenic boat ride.
- Explore the town of St. Gilgen and take the Zwölferhorn cable car.
- Visit the town of Hallstatt and take a boat trip on Hallstättersee.
- Enjoy a scenic drive through the Salzkammergut region.

MAPS

Austria Map

Salzburg City Map

Salzburg Walking Tour Map

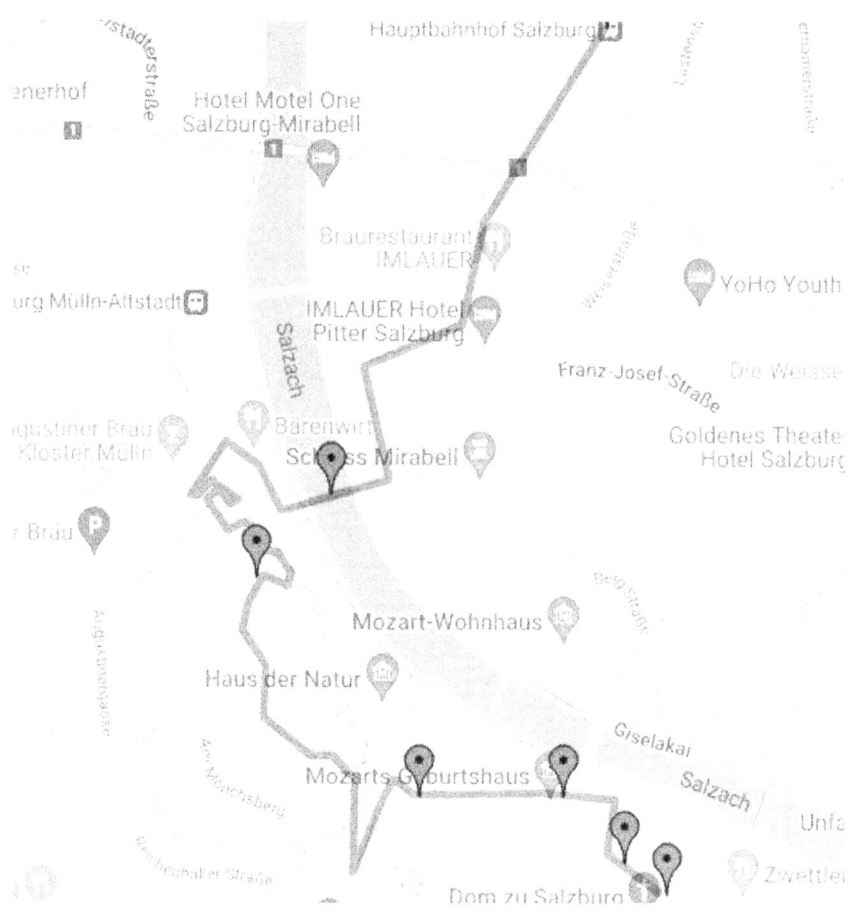

Sound of Music Movie Locations Map

Salzburg Food Market Map

Salzburg Accommodation Map

CONCLUSION

As your time in Salzburg draws to a close, we hope that this travel guide has enriched your visit to Mozart's beloved hometown. From exploring its historic landmarks, meandering through its enchanting streets, to immersing yourself in its vibrant cultural scene, Salzburg offers a delightful tapestry of experiences.

May the echoes of Mozart's music continue to resonate in your heart, reminding you of the artistic legacy that permeates every corner of this remarkable city. Whether you've wandered through its palaces, climbed its fortress, or savored the flavors of its culinary delights, Salzburg leaves an indelible mark on the soul of every traveler.

As you bid farewell to this enchanting destination, carry with you the memories of its timeless beauty and the magic of Mozart's melodies. Until we meet again in the embrace of Salzburg's timeless charm, safe travels and Auf Wiedersehen!

INDEX

Accommodation in Salzburg   13

Almkanal   64

Architecture and History   77

Attend a Festive Event   50

Baroque and Art Lover's Delight   121

Best Restaurants   57

Best Time to Visit Salzburg   9

Boat Rides   40

Budget-Friendly Travel Tips   116

Café Bazar   105

Classical Music Scene   72

Coffeehouse Culture   55

Cultural Events and Festivals   80

Currency and Payments   18

Day Trip to the Lakes and Mountains   122

Dreifaltigkeitskirche (Holy Trinity Church)   112

Electrical Outlets   22

Emergency Numbers   22

Family Fun Day   121

Family-Friendly Activities   46

Getting Around Salzburg   11

Gorges   65

Gwandhaus   109

Health and Safety   16

Hellbrunn Palace and Trick Fountains   35

Hohensalzburg Fortress   27

How to Get to Salzburg   10

Internet and Communication   24

Kaffee-Alchemie   111

Kapitelplatz and Giant Chess Board   38

Language   21

Linzer Gasse   108

Local Customs and Etiquette   22

Local Insights   115

Mirabell Palace and Gardens   29

Mozart Heritage Tour   120

Mozart's Birthplace (Mozarts Geburtshaus)   87

Mozarts Geburtshaus (Mozart's Birthplace)   32

Mozart's Legacy   69

Mozart's Residence (Mozarts Wohnhaus)   89

Mozarts Wohnhaus (Mozart's Residence)   34

Mozartsteg Pedestrian Bridge   106

Müllner Bräu Brewery & Beer Garden   102

Museum der Moderne Salzburg (Museum of Modern Art)   84

Museums and Galleries   79

Musical Journey through Salzburg   122

Nature and Hiking Expedition   120

Nightlife in Salzburg   44

Nonnberg Abbey   100

Outdoor Activities   43

Packing Essentials 19

Panorama Museum Salzburg 92

Parks and Gardens 62

Petersfriedhof Cemetery 99

Rivers 64

Safety Tips 114

Salzach River 64

Salzburg Accommodation Map 127

Salzburg Baroque Museum 94

Salzburg by Night 121

Salzburg Cathedral (Salzburger Dom) 30

Salzburg Cathedral Museum (Dommuseum Salzburg) 90

Salzburg City Map 123

Salzburg Cuisine 54

Salzburg Culinary Experience 121

Salzburg Festival 71

Salzburg Food Market Map 126

Salzburg Marionette Theater   74

Salzburg Mountains and Hills   60

Salzburg Museum   85

Salzburg Old Town (Altstadt)   26

Salzburg Old Town Walking Tour 120

Salzburg Walking Tour Map   124

Salzburg's Cultural Heritage Sites 82

Salzburg's Lakes   59

Shopping   48

Shopping in Salzburg   14

Solo Travel Tips in Salzburg   118

Sound of Music Movie Locations Map   125

Sound of Music Tour   120

St. Peter's Abbey and Cemetery   37

St. Peter's Abbey Museum (Stift St. Peter)   97

Stieglkeller   103

Strolls and Hikes   51

Take a Day Trip   41

Toy Museum (Spielzeugmuseum) 95

Traditional Folk Music   75

Travel Insurance   19

Visa and Travel Documents for Austria   8

Visit Christmas Markets   47

Waterfalls   67

Printed in Great Britain
by Amazon